BREAK TIME

LOGIC PUZZLES

?

k

Kandour Ltd

Published by
Kandour Ltd
1-3 Colebrooke Place
London
N1 8HZ
UNITED KINGDOM

This edition printed in 2006
for Bookmart Ltd
Registered Number 2372865
Trading as Bookmart Ltd
Blaby Road
Wigston
Leicester LE18 4SE

First published 2006

10 9 8 7 6 5 4 3 2 1

Author: Tiger Wisbey
Editor: Tammy Seto
Design and Layout: Alexander Rose Publishing Limited
Production: Carol Titchener

Printed and bound in Denmark
by Nørhaven Paperback A/S

ISBN-10: 1-905741-09-X

ISBN-13: 978-1-905741-09-0

How to solve...

udoku

l in the grid so that every column, row and 3x3 box ntain the numbers 1 to 9.

akuro

l in the grid so that each run of squares adds up to the tal in the box above or to the left. Only use the numbers o 9 and never use the same numbers twice, in that run he same numbers may be used in a different run)

odoku

l in the grid so that every column, row and 3x3 box ntain the letters A to I.

Easy Sudoku

8	4	3	9					7
	9			7	1	8		4
		7		5				3
	5			6	8	9		
7	6						4	
					7	5		6
2		8	6			4		
4					3			5
6					9	2		

Easy Sudoku

5	4	1		8			6	
	8		1			7	4	9
6			2	3				
2	9							6
				4	2	8		
	1			7		9		5
	6					1		4
4		5				2		
		7			5		3	

Easy Sudoku

5	2		8	6		9		
		8		2	7		5	
	1	7	3				2	8
3					6	7	1	
	4			5	2			9
7		2			9			
		4			8	5		6
		5			4		3	
2	7						4	

Easy Sudoku

4	2	7	6	9	8	5		3
3				4	5	7	6	2
1					3	4		
		4	3			8		
		2					9	
	7				9			
	9		8	5	2	3		
				6				
8	6	5	9			1		

Easy Sudoku

1	2				6			7
3		8	4	7				
	9	4		1		6		
	8	6	9			1		
4	1				8		9	
		7		2	1			4
5					4	3	2	8
6		1			5			9
	4				3	5		

Easy Sudoku

4			1				3	
		2		4			5	6
3					7			8
5	7	3						1
	1	4		8		3		
8			3		5	4		
9	6					5	1	2
1		8					7	4
2			6					

Easy Sudoku

6					4			
1	2			9	3			5
	4		1	2				
	5	2	8					
		1	3			5	7	
7	3	4			2	6	9	
	7		2		6			1
5	8		9					
		3		7	5	9	8	

Easy Sudoku

7			2		6	4	9	
6	1	4		3				
8						6		
	7	1		2		8		
		5	6	7	9			
9	3				1		7	
	4	7	3					
					4		2	7
1				8			3	

Easy Sudoku

5		2			3			4
9	3				7			
1			8					
		5		7	8		3	
	1		3				8	
			4		9	5	6	
		3	9			1		
2	7	1	5		6	8		
4	6							

Easy Sudoku

1		8					5	3
6	2	9	3				8	
					1			
2	1	5						9
		3	5		4	2		
	9	6			3			
8	5		9			1	2	
			8	1	7	6		
							9	

Easy Sudoku

4	9	6		1	7	5		
	8	3				9		
				8		7		4
	3	8					4	
6			7		4			2
			2	6			9	
		7	9		3		6	1
	5		1	7	6			9

Easy Sudoku

9	4	6	7		2			3
		7			1		6	
				9		7		5
1		8	4					2
	2							6
4				3	7	5		
	5	4						7
		3		8				
2	8		3			9		

Easy Sudoku

4					7	5		
		9	1	2				
8	1	2	4					
6				4	2			
7		1	9	6			4	5
	4	8			1		3	6
9						8		1
	2		6	8			5	7
						4	2	9

Easy Sudoku

1	7	5	2					
	6				9			
4		2		1	6			
			9		3		7	
	2	4		6		8	9	
6			7				1	
8	4	6				9		
	1						6	
		3			1		4	

Easy Sudoku

4		2				1		8
6	7	9		8			4	5
8	1		9		5	6		
					8			9
		6					1	3
	9			1			5	4
9			7		2			1
2	8		1					
	4			9	6		7	

Easy Sudoku

1	5		9				2	
8					4			7
2		4	3	8				
	1			7		5		3
		5				7		
3			2		1			
7			4			8	3	
4		9						
	6	8	7	3	2		9	

Easy Sudoku

3	8	1						6
5	9	6	1			7		
	4			8	9			
8		9			7	3	5	
7	1	5		9				
	3			1	8			
	7	8		2	1		6	
					5	9	1	
		4			3	2		

18

Easy Sudoku

6		8		4		7	2	
		7	2	3		6		
1			9					
4		9		7		8		
					2		5	
7	8		5		6	1	4	
	7			2	4		9	
	4						8	5
2								

Easy Sudoku

9		7		3	6	8	2	
	1	6	7				5	
				2			6	
1	6	9	8		2	5		
				9				
4		2	1			7	9	
3				1	7			
						9	4	3
8	2	4			9			

Easy Sudoku

4		3					8	
	7		3		9		4	
6			1			5		7
7		8	4	9				
9		5		2		6		
				6	7			
				7			2	3
8	9		2		4	1		
	4							

Easy Sudoku

1							9	4
		4	9		6	3		
8		3	7	4				2
			5	7	4	6	1	
9					1	8		
			8	2			7	
			1					
4		9	2					
7	5			9			8	

Easy Sudoku

4	8			5	1		2	
		2						4
3	5	7		8				
7	9				8		6	1
1			2			3	4	
8							9	
		6	1					9
	4			3				2
				6	4			

Easy Sudoku

7	8		2					
	9		6			3		
6		4		8	9		7	
				5				1
	7	3				6	4	
		5	9	3		7		
	4	9		7			6	
3			4			2		9
1	6					4		

Easy Sudoku

2	8		7	5			3	
3	5		8			4		1
6		1	2		4	7		
					5			
1	4	8	3	6	7			2
				8				
	6	2			8	3	1	
7		9		2	3		8	
								4

Easy Sudoku

8	6			1				
	9			2	3			
		5	4			1		
9				8				2
1	2	3				4		
							9	
		2	8		6		7	
	8						1	
3	5	7	1	9		8	4	

Easy Sudoku

2		7	5	9				8
1	3	6	4			5		9
		5				3		7
		9	6		1	7	5	4
4					2			6
6						1		
	6		2			4		5
	9			6	7			
7				5		9		

Easy Sudoku

1	2	6		9				
		5	7				1	3
			6					
4			5	8		7		9
3	5		4					1
			2	7		4		
	6	3	8				9	
		8				5	7	
				4	6		2	

Easy Sudoku

5	3		4	2				9
	4				3		8	
		2			9			5
7					8			6
3			2					7
	6	1				5		
9		6	8	4		1	3	
		7			2			
	8		5		6			

Easy Sudoku

5	6		4		9		2	
					1	4	8	
			6	2				5
3	7			9			1	
8		1	5	3				2
					4		3	
6	5					2	4	
		3				7	5	
4		7		1				

Easy Sudoku

9	3			4				
1		5		8	7			
	8	7	3		9	1		
		9			4	3		1
4	6	3			5		7	
7	1		9		3		4	
						7	9	5
		6			1			
	9	4				6		

Easy Sudoku

3	2	6	7		1	8	9	
1			6				3	
					5			6
	3	1	8		6	2		
					4	7	8	1
7					2			
				9				2
9	1	3			8			
			1	6				

Easy Sudoku

8		3	1	4	5	9	6	
				6		1	8	
	7			2			4	
9				1	8		5	
1		5	9				7	6
2					6			
		6	4					
5		2	7		1			9
					3	5		

Easy Sudoku

9				8			5	
		3	5	7			9	
	4				9	8		
1	6				7			9
						6	7	
5	9		3		1			4
	8							
			2	5	3	7		
		6	4			3		

Easy Sudoku

9	2	5			6			7
3	1	4	5	7	8		2	
	7		3				1	
				8	5	2	4	1
						5		9
		9					6	
		7	4				8	
8	6		2	3	9			
				6				

Easy Sudoku

8		9			1			3
		7		4	2	5		
1	2				3	7		
2	4		8			3	5	6
	6		1	3			9	
9				5	8	1	3	
3			2		7		8	

Easy Sudoku

9	3	6		5				7
8			2		7			
2	5			4		3		
	4							
1		9	5	8	2		3	
6			3					
		1			6			
3	2		4				6	
4			9	7		2		8

Easy Sudoku

9	3	1		4		2	6	8
	2	7		8		3		
			1			4		9
5					1			2
1			2	3	6		4	
			4				1	
6				1				
	9		8					7
2			9		4	8		

Easy Sudoku

1		8			4		5	
4			5		9			2
5	7			1	2		4	
2	5		3			8		
		7						
	8	4		5	7			1
7			4	2				9
		5		6		1		
	6				5			

Easy Sudoku

2	4		8	3		9		7
	9	6		1				
				4	2			3
	6	3	5		7	1	8	9
8		5	3	6			2	
		9						5
			2			4		1
					1	8		
	8	4		7				

Easy Sudoku

2	9	4	8					
		5		9				2
3	7	8	2		4	9		
9			1		7		5	
4			3			6	7	
7				2	6	3		
	6	7				4	9	8
	4				8			3
				4				

Easy Sudoku

4	9		7			2		8
	2			3	4	9		5
		7		2			4	
	7	2	6					3
5		4				6		
				7	8		1	
		8	3			7	5	9
7	6		5	4				1
		9						

Easy Sudoku

1	3	7		4				9
				3		7	8	
6				7		3	1	
	7		4	2			6	8
8		9						
				9	1	5	7	
7							2	
	2	4	6	8	3		9	
	8		7		2			

Easy Sudoku

8	5			4	1		2	3
6		9		8				
				3	9	5		
			1	6		8	3	5
	8			2			7	
4								
	9	3	4		7	6	8	
	4		8					
7					3	1	4	

Easy Sudoku

8	1	5	2				3	
9	6					1	8	
					3			6
		8					9	
2	3	6		4				
4			7	6			2	
3			1	5	9			8
5		2				3		
			4			5		

Easy Sudoku

9	2		1					
1		5	7				6	
				2			3	4
	6	3		7		8		5
						3	1	
		2	5			7		
				8		9	5	3
7					9			8
	8		4					

Easy Sudoku

3				9				
2						3	7	
5	6		2		4			
				1	9	7		4
	3				7	1		
7			4		5		2	
6						2	1	8
	2	3						
4	9		1	6		5		

Easy Sudoku

5	6				2	8		
	2		4	5	8	9		6
3				9	7			2
2	5					1	8	
		1			3			7
			1					9
8		6	7				4	
9				2	4			
	3			6				

Easy Sudoku

8				2			7	
								9
9	6	2			8	3		
1		8	6	3			9	
5						6	2	
	4	6	1					
			2		7	4	5	
			4					
		9	5	6		8		

Easy Sudoku

2		1		4	7	9		
					8		6	7
	6		2	9			3	
	7		5	8				2
5			4				8	1
	1		3	6				
6							9	5
9						4		3
						7		

Easy Sudoku

9			4	6		5		3
		4		5		1		2
	5	7		8	3			
		6			8		9	
3		1			4	2		
			1	3		6		
	8							
	1				6	9		
		3	9		7		1	

Easy Sudoku

9		6			7	1	4	
	8	2		1		3		
1				8	9		5	7
5		8			4	9		
				6				2
			2		8			
			1		2	4	7	
	9						1	
4	1	5	9		6			

Easy Sudoku

6		9		2	8			
	2			1	5		6	
3	5			7	4	2		
4				6				
1				8		6		2
					1	8	9	
					3	7		6
7	4		1		6			
9					7	1	3	

Easy Sudoku

4		1		8	9	7	2	
3		5				8		6
8			4					1
	3		5			2	6	
6	4		7	9			5	
	7	8	6	2				
				6		3		
	8			3				2
			9					

Easy Sudoku

8		3	9	1				
		9					6	1
	5			3	6			4
	3		8			2	1	9
2			3				7	5
7		1						
				8	3	7		
6				7		9	4	
		5		4			8	

Easy Sudoku

7		4					5	8
	6		9			1		
	5			7			3	
4		2	6				8	1
1				8	3		6	
3			2					
		8				6		
5			8	6			1	4
		7	3	9	1			

Easy Sudoku

9							5	7
	1		9	3	7	6		
	6			1				
1			2	5			4	9
	8			9	3	7		
2	3		6					
				6			8	
					1	4		
7		1	4				3	

Easy Sudoku

2		9	8			6		3
	5			4			8	2
				7		9		
					6		5	1
	9		1	8	2			7
	7	2	4					
	2	7				5		
3			9		4		2	
4	1						9	

Easy Sudoku

8			4	9	3		1	6
6	3			1		8		4
					2			
2		8	1			5	9	
5	4					1		7
		1			6		4	
					1			
	2	6	8	4		9		
4		7		3				

Easy Sudoku

6	1					2	4	
8			2		4	6		
	9					3		1
9		6	3		8			
		3	7	4			9	
			5					
	6	1		7				
5					2	7	6	
2			9			1		

Easy Sudoku

5			6		8		1	3
3		2		1	7			
	4		2	9				7
	6		3			5	7	8
						9	3	
7					6			
6		3			9			
	1			6			9	
9	7	5						

Easy Sudoku

7							8	
	5				1	2	6	
8			3	9	2	7		
5					3	1	9	
9				5	4			2
1	8			7			5	
		7				4		9
		8	9		6			
3			2					

Easy Sudoku

6	1	9						
7			1	6	4			3
		5				6		
	5				6	9	2	1
	9	7	8	5				
2		4	9		1	7	8	
9						4		
	3		6	9	8	2		
	2		3					

Easy Sudoku

6	9	3		2				
				1			8	3
5		1			3	2		
	2		9			1	3	
		8	1				6	
	3		6	8	7	5	9	
	6	9	2	5				
	4			6				1
					8			

Easy Sudoku

2	8	4		1	5		9	6
					9			
5			7	8	4	1		
			4		1		6	
3					2		1	
	5		6				3	9
	9	5			7		4	
7							5	
8	4		1					

Easy Sudoku

1		6		2	4			
8	4				5		1	
	2					4		
4			1	3		2	5	
2			9		8	1		
5	6			4			9	
3		8				5	7	1
						3	8	4
			3					

Easy Sudoku

8		9		2		6		
				4	1	9		7
			6		9	4		
						1		6
	5	4					7	
9	3			5				
				7		2	1	
5	2	3	9					
6	1			8				

Easy Sudoku

8			1	6		3		7
	9		3				5	
	5		8		9	2		
9		7			4			5
	3	2		9	6		7	
4								
		8		5		6	3	
5			6		8		4	
				1				

Easy Sudoku

4	5		3			7		2
	1		8				3	5
				9				6
1			5					
7	8			1		5		
2			9		6			
5				3	8	6		
8	6	1						
		7			2	4	1	

Easy Sudoku

6		2	8	5	3			
							9	2
	7	8	2		4	3		6
			1		6	9	3	
	2						4	7
5	1						2	
		1	4	6				
8			7					1
4			5		9			

Easy Sudoku

6					3			
		2		5	6			3
8		4	9	7				2
	2	5		1	7			8
3	4			2	5	9	7	
7	1					6		
				4	2			
		1			8		4	
		7					5	

Easy Sudoku

9		3				6		2
4	5	1	6			7		9
		7	5		3			
					4	9	2	5
	3			7			4	
	9				2			
				5		4	8	
1				8				
2	6		3		1			

Easy Sudoku

5	1	3	8			7		6
6			1					
				3	2			
		4		1			8	3
	6				8	4	1	
9				4	5			7
8	3					6	5	
						9		
2	5		7			8		

Easy Sudoku

4		6	9			2		8
	7		1			4		
5	9			3	8	6		
7		3		1				
		5		7		3		
				8	9		4	7
8	3	4					2	
				2		9	6	
2					5			

Easy Sudoku

7	9		1	2		8	3	
							4	
2	4		3		9		6	
	6			3				
	3			4	5	7	2	8
		7			2	3	9	
3					1			
5		4		6	8	9		
	2	9		7		4		

Easy Sudoku

6		5		2	8			9
		7					5	8
	2			7	9	3		
	1						6	
	6	3	4	9	7			1
4	7			6				
9			6					5
	4							
		1		8	2			

Easy Sudoku

3			7			8		2
		6	9		5	4		
							6	
5						6	4	
					2			8
7	4				1	5		
		5		9			7	
9	7		2	6	8	3		
1			5	3		9		

Easy Sudoku

4	5		3				7	2
								5
	1	3	2		7			4
	7	6		2			1	8
8			4		1			6
		4			6			
2			1			5		3
			6	4	5	8		
						9		

78

Easy Sudoku

7	1	2	8	9				
4			2				7	3
						9		
8							5	
3		1	6	8	5			
	7	9	3		1			
	3	4		7		1	8	
	6		9			4	2	
2				6				

Easy Sudoku

7		4			5	1		3
8		2				5		7
	9		4					
4	7			6		3		
6	3				9			
		5	1	8				
			2			7	3	
	5				7	8	2	
	8			5			6	

Easy Sudoku

3			5	4			1	2
	6		7	8			5	
	7		2	3		6	8	
	2		4	6				
		4	8		3			6
	8		9		2		7	
				7	5		6	
	3							
1		6	3	9		8		

Easy Sudoku

5	3				9		4	
4			1	3	6			2
		6		8			9	
		2	5				1	8
3		4		1				
9			7	4		2		6
			8		7	1		
6		9			4			5
		5		6				

Easy Sudoku

5	4	8	3	6	9			1
		1		7			4	5
7		9	1			3		
6	9	5					2	
								9
				5	7		8	
8	7	6				1	3	
			6				5	
2		3		8		4		

Easy Sudoku

2			9		8	5	7	
4				3	7			
3							2	
5		3	6	9			1	2
6	9				2	8		
	4	2	7					6
7			5	6			3	
9		6				4	5	7
					1			

Easy Sudoku

3	1	5			8	2	4	
			9					5
6			3					
	4	1		2				6
	2	9					8	3
		6		9	7	4		
	5		7	8			2	
					5	8		
	8	3	1	4		5		

Easy Sudoku

7	2				1			
9			2	8	7			6
4					3		1	2
		6			8		5	7
	4		6				3	
	3		9	1			6	
1			7				2	4
					4			1
6	8					3		

Easy Sudoku

4				5		8	3	2
		1					9	4
9	2		7				1	
	3			1				5
1			5	6			4	
5					7		6	
6	7				1	4		9
		4	9			6		
3				8		2		

Easy Sudoku

9			6			2		8
	4			9	5	3		
6		8			4			
	2		3				1	5
	9			2	1			
4		1				9		
		7		8		4	5	
		9		7		8		2
					3		6	

Easy Sudoku

7	3	1				6		
8			5	2	6		1	
2						8		4
9				7			4	5
	4		9	5				8
	2	8		4	1			
3	8		7		9			6
6				8		3		9
	7					5		

Easy Sudoku

5		9					8	
1	8		3			9		6
		4	6	8				1
3				1		4		
		2	5		3			
	1		2	7		3		
7				5		1		4
	4		1		2	7		
6				3		8		

Easy Sudoku

8	1	4			7			6
9	2			3				
3		7	2	4				1
		8	6	1	9		5	
5			8		4		1	
	7					9	4	
7		5			2			
			5	6				7
2						4		

Medium Sudoku

9		3				6		2
4	5	1	6			7		9
		7	5		3			
					4	9	2	5
	3			7			4	
	9				2			
				5		4	8	
1				8				
2	6		3		1			

Medium Sudoku

5	1	3	8			7		6
6			1					
				3	2			
		4		1			8	3
	6				8	4	1	
9				4	5			7
8	3					6	5	
						9		
2	5		7			8		

Medium Sudoku

4		6	9			2		8
	7		1			4		
5	9			3	8	6		
7		3		1				
		5		7		3		
				8	9		4	7
8	3	4					2	
				2		9	6	
2					5			

Medium Sudoku

7	9		1	2		8	3	
							4	
2	4		3		9		6	
	6			3				
	3			4	5	7	2	8
		7			2	3	9	
3					1			
5		4		6	8	9		
	2	9		7		4		

Medium Sudoku

6		5		2	8			9
		7					5	8
	2			7	9	3		
	1						6	
	6	3	4	9	7			1
4	7			6				
9			6					5
	4							
		1		8	2			

Medium Sudoku

3			7			8		2
		6	9		5	4		
							6	
5						6	4	
					2			8
7	4				1	5		
		5		9			7	
9	7		2	6	8	3		
1			5	3		9		

7

Medium Sudoku

7	1	2	8	9				
4			2				7	3
						9		
8							5	
3		1	6	8	5			
	7	9	3		1			
	3	4		7		1	8	
	6		9			4	2	
2				6				

Medium Sudoku

4	5		3				7	2
								5
	1	3	2		7			4
	7	6		2			1	8
8			4		1			6
		4			6			
2			1			5		3
			6	4	5	8		
						9		

Medium Sudoku

7		4			5	1		3
8		2				5		7
	9		4					
4	7			6		3		
6	3				9			
		5	1	8				
			2			7	3	
	5				7	8	2	
	8			5			6	

10

Medium Sudoku

3			5	4			1	2
	6		7	8			5	
	7		2	3		6	8	
	2		4	6				
		4	8		3			6
	8		9		2		7	
				7	5		6	
	3							
1		6	3	9		8		

11

Medium Sudoku

5	3				9		4	
4			1	3	6			2
		6		8			9	
		2	5				1	8
3		4		1				
9			7	4		2		6
			8		7	1		
6		9			4			5
		5		6				

Medium Sudoku

1		4	9				8	
	5			3				4
8	7	9		1				
	1	3	2	4				8
		8	5	7		1	9	
7	9				1			
6					4		3	
	2		3	5				
			8		6	7		

Medium Sudoku

5	4	8	3	6	9			1
		1		7			4	5
7		9	1			3		
6	9	5					2	
								9
				5	7		8	
8	7	6				1	3	
			6				5	
2		3		8		4		

Medium Sudoku

2			9		8	5	7	
4				3	7			
3							2	
5		3	6	9			1	2
6	9				2	8		
	4	2	7					6
7			5	6			3	
9		6				4	5	7
					1			

Medium Sudoku

3	1	5			8	2	4	
			9					5
6			3					
	4	1		2				6
	2	9					8	3
		6		9	7	4		
	5		7	8			2	
					5	8		
	8	3	1	4		5		

Medium Sudoku

7	2				1			
9			2	8	7			6
4					3		1	2
		6			8		5	7
	4		6				3	
	3		9	1			6	
1			7				2	4
					4			1
6	8					3		

Medium Sudoku

4				5		8	3	2
		1					9	4
9	2		7				1	
	3			1				5
1			5	6			4	
5					7		6	
6	7				1	4		9
		4	9			6		
3				8		2		

Medium Sudoku

9			6			2		8
	4			9	5	3		
6		8			4			
	2		3				1	5
	9			2	1			
4		1				9		
		7		8		4	5	
		9		7		8		2
					3		6	

19

Medium Sudoku

7	3	1				6		
8			5	2	6		1	
2						8		4
9				7			4	5
	4		9	5				8
	2	8		4	1			
3	8		7		9			6
6				8		3		9
	7					5		

Medium Sudoku

5		9					8	
1	8		3			9		6
		4	6	8				1
3				1		4		
		2	5		3			
	1		2	7		3		
7				5		1		4
	4		1		2	7		
6				3		8		

21

Medium Sudoku

8	1	4			7			6
9	2			3				
3		7	2	4				1
		8	6	1	9		5	
5			8		4		1	
	7					9	4	
7		5			2			
			5	6				7
2						4		

22

Medium Sudoku

3		8	2		9	4		1
	4	9	3	6			2	8
1	6			5		7		
		3		1				6
	7				6		9	4
5	1		6			9		7
8					7	2		
			8					

Medium Sudoku

5		2				7		4
4								8
		1	4	6			3	5
		4		1	6	3	8	
7			2	3	5	6		
2							7	
					9		5	
	8		5					6
			3	2		9		

Medium Sudoku

3		5	8			6		1
	2	7						5
6			7	3		2		
4	5			7		3		8
		1	2	4		7		
			5	8				6
				9			4	
	9	6				1		3
	8	4			2			

Medium Sudoku

7	6				3		1	
	8		4			5	6	
	5	9	2	1			7	
			5		1	6	4	9
		4	6	7	8	2		5
6			9			7		
1	9			3				
	7	8			5			3

Medium Sudoku

6	4			9				
	2		8		7		5	
5	7	1	2		4			
	5					1		4
	8	3					9	
	1		3		2			
					3	9		
			5			6	8	7
2	9			1				

Medium Sudoku

7	9			1	5	4		
6		8	9				1	3
	1	2		6	4			
			1		7		3	
	2			9	3	6	7	
9							4	
	7							
	5	6		4			9	1
4		1	2	5				

Medium Sudoku

8		5			1			2
				8	2			
	4	6		9				1
					4	9	1	
7	5		9	3				8
1	9	4	2	7			3	5
			3	6				
	3	7				8		

Medium Sudoku

2	9	4	8				7	5
5						1	3	
	7			6	9			4
	1	7	9		8			
	6				3			8
3				7	2			
			7				9	3
		5						
8				1	4		6	

Medium Sudoku

8		6			1	2	9	
7	3			6			4	
	1	5	3					
9			8				3	7
	7	2		1				
		3						6
	6	1	5	9			8	
					2	3	1	
						4		

31

Medium Sudoku

5					2	6		4
		8	3					1
	4	3				9		
			6			1		
3	9				5	7		
	5	1	7	2				
		6	5	8	4			
4	2			6				
		5		3		4	9	

Medium Sudoku

4		7	6					
		6		1	2		3	8
					3			
8	9		1	7			5	
		3				6		9
2				8		1		
		9	2					
5	2		4			9	1	
6								

Medium Sudoku

6			3	4		5		
5	7	4				6	3	
9	3		7			4		2
7	9	2			1			6
				6	8	7		3
		6			5		1	
	5							7
2			6					
4				2				

Medium Sudoku

7	9	2	6	1				5
3		8		5				
				7	3		2	4
			3				9	
	7					6	1	
2	5	1						
	3		5	4	8		7	9
			9			1		
				6			8	

35

Medium Sudoku

2	4	7				3		
	6				1	5	9	2
							7	
3	7		8			2		9
			3			6		7
1	9		6	4		8		5
5		4						
	8		7		3			
	3		5	8		9		

Medium Sudoku

3	8			4	9		6	
		6		3	1	7	9	
	9							5
4			8	2				
				7	3	5		4
		3	1				2	
			2					7
		8		5		1		
1	5	7	3		6			

Medium Sudoku

5		9	8				7	6
				1	9		5	8
		3		6	7			
				7	1		6	2
6			4			8		
	3	5						7
	5				2			
8		2					4	1
7		4	1	8			3	

38

Medium Sudoku

7		4						
8				6		1	3	
9							4	5
				1	2		6	8
				3	9		7	1
	2			5		3		
6	7	5		2	1		8	
	8				7	6		2
	4	1		9	6			

Medium Sudoku

1				5	4			
9			3	6	8			1
	4				7			9
7						8	9	
6						7	4	3
	3	2				6		
	1		7	4		9		
			8		5	3		
5		7	2	9			6	

Medium Sudoku

2	3			5		6	4	9
9				2		5		3
		5				7		
		8		4			2	
6	5		1	9			3	
4			2	8				6
		1		6		2		8
7								
	9		5					

Medium Sudoku

7		1			3	8	2	
		4		8	1			6
5				9	2	7		
3		9		1	6			
			3			6	9	1
				4			3	7
8	1					5		9
9		5		7				
	2		9	3				8

Medium Sudoku

4	5				1			3
	9	7		6			1	
8			4		5	9		
			2	5			6	
7			9	3				
3		9	8					2
5	3	4					8	
		2	1	8		4		

Medium Sudoku

2	1	5		3				7
	8	3	4	9	5	1		
4	9		1		7		8	
		8	5	4	3			
			6					
	5	7	9				6	
		4	7			2	3	9
						4	1	5
		9						

Medium Sudoku

6				4	2			
	4	9		1		6		2
7	1				3	9		
			8			1		7
8	6		7					9
	3			5	6			
	7	3	2	6		4		
		5				3		
					8	2	5	

Medium Sudoku

7					9		4	
6	8	2		1	4			3
	1		8	7		5	2	
8	9					1	5	4
	5	1		9				8
			9		5			
4	6		2	8				
		8	3			2		

Medium Sudoku

9			3			1	7	
		4			9	2		
6	7	8					3	
7	6		1	2				
			7	4				
2		3	8		6		5	
	1	7			8		2	
8		5			1	4		
	9			5		8		

Medium Sudoku

7	8		4		5	2		6
9			7					
		6	3		1		7	
6					4		3	2
	3					8		
		2	5					7
1	9	8	2		3			
	5		9	7			8	
3			1	5	8	9		

Medium Sudoku

5	4	9		2			8	
1			9	7		2	4	
	6		3			9		
3		2	5				6	
6		5			8			7
8	1				3		9	
				5		3		8
	3		1		7			
						4	1	

Medium Sudoku

4	6	2				9		3
	1							
8		3		4	5	1		
			5				1	
	3		8	7				2
6		9	3					
9				3		5	7	1
	8				9			4
7		4		2		8		

Medium Sudoku

7	3	5		4	8		9	1
			5		1			
6				7			4	
			4					
1		2	6			4	7	
		7	9	1		8		
9				2		3	8	
	1			3	4			
2	7					5		

Medium Sudoku

4	3			1	9	7		2
	6					3	9	
8			3			6		1
2							6	8
1	5							4
	8	6		9	2	5		
5		7		4	3			
	2	3	1		8			9
	4						7	

Medium Sudoku

8	3					1	2	
			6			7		3
7					4			
	2				1	8		
	4	7			2	6		
3		8	7	6				1
5			9	8	6			
		1		7			5	6
2				4			8	

Medium Sudoku

9	8		4			6		
			3	6				1
5				7	8		4	
	6		5		1			
7								8
	5	4	6	2				3
	3			5	2			
	9	2	1	4				
4						1		

Medium Sudoku

8	7	4	3		2			
1	9	2	4		6			
	6		7					
	1	7	2			5		
2		8		4				
				1	9	3	2	
7			1	3		8	5	
3	4					1	7	
			9				3	2

Medium Sudoku

9		5			7		8	
			6	1		3		
3		1		8		5		
4			7			6	9	
				6	1		7	4
2	7							3
								8
6	9	3		7				
7				3	2		6	

Medium Sudoku

2				3		1		6
		5	2					
6	7				5	9		3
4	8					2		
			4		7		8	
	3	9		1				4
	4		3	7		6		
	5				9		4	
		7		2	4			

Medium Sudoku

4	1	3	7				6	9
	2	7	1			3	4	
			2	3		7		
7				2	5	6	9	
	4						2	
9	6				1			
			4		3	8	7	
	9	8			7			6
								5

Medium Sudoku

8							3	7
	6	9		1				4
1		7	8		5			
				6	9	2		5
			7			3		
		2		8		6		1
		8		7		5		
7	5	1	6	9			8	2
	9	4						

Medium Sudoku

1		6	7	8	9			3
7		2		1		9		
					6			1
	9		5					7
		5		3		8		
	4	7	1			3	2	
	6	1	9	7	5			
4							6	
		9			4			

Medium Sudoku

5		3	6	7	1			
	1			4	9	2		5
	8	9	5		3		6	
7	4							2
	3					4		
		6		3		7		
2	6	8					4	
1		5	4	6			2	
			1					

61

Medium Sudoku

1		5			6	8		7
6	4			2				1
			1		9		5	
					2	5	8	4
9				5				
			6	8		2		
2		9				3		
3	1		5			6		
5	6	4			1	7		

Medium Sudoku

8	9		7	1		4		3
	5	7	6	2				1
	2							
5	8				6			4
		9			8		6	2
	7					9	3	
9	1			5				
		3	4		9	1	7	
			2					

Medium Sudoku

9			6	4				
	6	2			3			
	4				2	5		9
8	5			9		4	3	
2			8					6
		7	1			8		
		6	4	8		7		
				2	7		9	
		9				2	8	

64

Medium Sudoku

3	6			2				
5	9	8	1		3	2		4
			6	8		9	3	
1	8		7					6
	3			4		1		
2			5	6			8	
4		1	3		7			
					8	4		
	2			5				

65

Medium Sudoku

9	8	4	2			7	3	
7		1	6					
		3		8	4			5
5	9					6		
		2	5	1		3		
				7	9	5	2	
6				2		1		
8	2			3				
1	3					2	9	

66

Medium Sudoku

1	3	5	8					
6		2						
4	7		9			5		
		6	2	3	4	8	7	
	8	7	1		9			6
9		3	6			1		
		9				6	5	3
8				6			1	2
							4	

Medium Sudoku

4	8	7			3		1	
9				6		3		8
					4	7		
	6	2			5		8	3
					1	4		
7				9			6	
	2	4				5	9	
		3			9			
5	9		7	2		8		

Medium Sudoku

7		4				9		6
	3					1		
8				3	4			
	4	7	9	5			1	
		3			1	8	6	
2	1			4		5		9
1				8	2	6		
					9			5
4		9		6	3			

Medium Sudoku

3	4				8			9
5		7	2			3	8	
			1			4	6	
		5			1		2	6
		9	7	2		8		
					5		1	
1	9			7			4	8
7				9				
8	2				4	6		

Medium Sudoku

3		6	8	2		7	4	
		9					3	
8	1		4				6	
	2			5	1		8	
					2			3
7		1		4		9		
6	8		1					4
2					6			
	3	5		8				

Medium Sudoku

4	5	7			2		8	1
		6	9	7		5	3	
9	8	3					6	
	4		8				2	5
	6						1	
			2		1	3		
			5		4			
1				2	7			
8			1	3				

Medium Sudoku

1								8
		4			2		5	
		9		3	5	2		7
8		6	2	7	3			
				4		6	2	
2	1	3		9	6		8	
3					9			
	2	7				9	6	
5		8		1	7			

73

Medium Sudoku

4	6		9			5	8	
8				3			9	4
		5			8	7		
				5	3			7
2		6	4			8		
3	9			1	6			5
5					4			6
6	8	4						
	1	3	5				2	

Medium Sudoku

5		1			2		9	4
	2				3		5	
6	3			7				
	8		7	5	4		3	
2			3		1	7		
	6	7	9					
	1						6	
			8				2	
	9		1					5

Medium Sudoku

4	3		2			9	1	7
	6						3	4
1		9				6		
9		6	3	5		1		
				1		3		6
	7				8		5	
6	1	4	8					
5					3			1
	9			6	2			

76

Medium Sudoku

7				2			3	9
8	1				9			6
9		4		6	8			
				7				
			8			7	4	3
		8	2		6	5		
5	3		4			6		
1		2				3	8	
6		7	5					

Medium Sudoku

8	5			1	3		7	6
	6			2			1	
		4	6			3	5	
1		9		4		2	3	
2	8				7	4	9	
								7
	2				5			8
6	3			8	4			
7			2	6				

78

Medium Sudoku

9		7			2		6	8
	8			4			7	
		6		8		9		
		5	1		8			6
			2	6			1	
	2	1			5		3	
	3			9	7			
1	7	8	5					
			8			3	5	

Medium Sudoku

1			3	8		7	9	
	7	4		5		8		2
5			2			3		
			1		8			7
6		2			3		4	
			6	9			5	
8	6						7	
2		1			6		8	
	9			1				

Medium Sudoku

4	1		6			2		9
8			3		9	7	4	
6				4	7			1
7		2			3			
9	5		7	6				
			1	8	2			7
	3				5	8		
								3
2	6		9		1			

Hard Sudoku

3					8	1		9
9			1				3	
8		2		3			6	
					4			6
		8			1	7		
	6	4	7			8		2
			8				7	
6				5		9		
	5	9				3		

Hard Sudoku

9				8	2			6
	8	5	7			9		
		6			3	5		
7			8		1		9	
	4	8	3	5			6	
			4		7		5	
						7		
2	9		1				8	4
5	6							

Hard Sudoku

6	2				4	8		
3		4			5	9	6	
	9		1	3				
	1		5	2		7	8	
							5	
4							9	
1			9		2	4	7	
5				7				
7		9						3

Hard Sudoku

5		8					6	2
4			5	9			1	3
3	7					4		
	9				1		7	
		1		6				8
	4		2	5				
9			3			5		
						6	3	
			4					

5

Hard Sudoku

5	7	3		1	9			4
			2	3				9
1				5			8	
		1			5	8	7	
				4				
		8					9	
3		5	4		6		1	
						3		7
7	8	6	1			5		

Hard Sudoku

2						3		9
6				3	2	1		
		3	4	6				8
3				8				7
7				1	6	5		
9	8				4			
	7	9	6		1	8		
5			8			7		
		6		4			2	

7

Hard Sudoku

5		3	1	6			2	
1							7	
7	2	8						9
	1			2				7
2			6	8		9	4	
		5						1
	5		9			4		
	4	1						
		6	4	1	2	3		

8

Hard Sudoku

5					9	6		4
3	4		5			8	9	
	9		4				5	2
					1	9		
	5	9	7	8			2	
8			3		6			
		3	6					5
1		4						
			9	4				

Hard Sudoku

6		7	3	2	8			
1	5						3	2
		3				4		
9			1		3			
2								
3		1		4	6	7	9	
	9		4					1
		2		8	9			3
		8						4

10

Hard Sudoku

1						9		
9		3	4				2	
	4	5	6			7		
			7				4	1
		2	8		5			
			2	4			5	7
		9			6		7	
	3	6						9
8	2			5		6		

Hard Sudoku

2				1			8	6
			7				9	4
3		9						2
4			5	6		8	1	3
1					8		5	
7						2		
	1						4	
	4		9	5				
	2		6			7		

Hard Sudoku

5					1	6		2
				5		7	9	
			4					
			9			8		
3		6		8	2		5	1
	9	2						4
	3	4	6	1				
2	6	7	5				3	
				9	3		6	

13

Hard Sudoku

8			2			5	7	
6		4	5		1			
		9	6				3	4
				5	2			
9				8	4			
1							4	
						7	8	9
3							2	1
4	8		9					5

Hard Sudoku

8		5		9			3	
7		4			2		8	9
	6			3		2		5
				8	3			4
		6			7			
3	7						2	
				6		5		
	4		8	5		7		
	1				9			

15

Hard Sudoku

6	5	8			9			
4	9		8	1				
				5	3			9
	8	4	7					6
5		1	4				2	
7					6	4		
	4		3	6		1		
		2		7			3	
			5	8				

16

Hard Sudoku

7	8				4	9		
1			5		6	7		
		4	7				2	
			4		8	5		1
			9				7	3
	5		1			4	6	
9								8
	2	8			5			
5	3			2			4	

17

Hard Sudoku

3		6		1		7		8
	1	5	8					
		9		5		1		
	2		6	4				
1				8	3	2		
7		8					6	
		2					7	3
5				6		4		
	3					5		9

Hard Sudoku

2			8			3	7	
	9	6	5				4	1
4		8		6	3	9		
								3
				8		6	9	
			2					
1	5	4		7				
8			6	9		5		
		3					8	

19

Hard Sudoku

6	2							
	5	1	2				8	
					6	4	1	
		7				3		9
	4			3	8	6	2	
			5	1			4	
				2	1		9	8
				7		1		
	6	8						

Hard Sudoku

6						2	9	5
	4	9				7	8	
5					3		6	1
		6		4		3		9
			2		5			7
		5		7				4
3	6	2						
	9	4		1	7			
		7	8					

Hard Sudoku

2		5			6			
1					3			8
6	3		5	4	7			1
			1			6		
				3	4		8	
	8			9			7	
	7	2		8				
		6		5	9		2	3
8					2			

Hard Sudoku

1	6			7			9	
	7		6	1		8	2	
		5	8		9	6	1	
	5				7		3	
3				2			5	
4		6						
		2	7	4			6	
						2	7	1
	3							

Hard Sudoku

7	6	9		4				
			7		6	5		9
2					1		6	
	7	8	9			1		2
4				1	7	6	5	
	5	1					9	
	4	3						
	2			7		8	3	
				2				

Hard Sudoku

8				4	5		3	
	1		7					5
			9		2	7	4	
7								3
	6	9	3				1	
1						2	6	4
		5	1	3		4		
	9			7				
2	8					9		

Hard Sudoku

9				1		7	2	
	1				2		5	
	8							
7					1		3	2
8	3		2		4			
			5	7				
3		1	7		5	9	8	
4		6	8			5		

Hard Sudoku

9		4				1		6
				6	3		4	
	5		1				8	
2	4						9	
3		5	4	7				
		7		3				
	3		6	5		9		
	8	6	3			5	2	
						6	7	

Hard Sudoku

6	3			2		5	4	
7			1				8	
					6	3		
		7						4
				5			6	
	4	2		7	9	8		
2			4		7		5	
		6		9	2		1	
	5	9	8	1				

Hard Sudoku

5			1	6	8	7		
4				2				1
	2		3	4		5		6
6	3				9			
	1	2	8					
7								9
	5		4				7	
	4		7	1	3	9		
				9	6		4	

Hard Sudoku

9			4			1		
4	5		8			7	2	
			9	6				
		1	5		6			
	4			7				1
3		5	2	9				
8	3		6	5	2	9		4
							7	3
6		4		3				5

Hard Sudoku

1			9		6		4	8
6	7				1	3		
4			5		8	6		
				5		8	2	
			4		9	1	5	
					2			
		1					3	7
5		9	1	8				
	6	2			4			

Hard Sudoku

9	6		4			1	3	
		7		6	8			9
	1		5	9			6	7
					2		8	
5	7							
2	3							
				1	4		2	
1						4		6
4		6		7			9	

Hard Sudoku

6	4	5					3	7
9			3			6		2
8					7			
1		2	5				9	
		7						1
				7	9	2		
							4	
4	1				8			6
2	5		6	3				

Hard Sudoku

2			5	6				1
	5			8	3		2	
8	9	3	1					6
		2						
	6		4		2		5	
	7		6			4		
	2	5						
			3	4			1	
				1		7	6	

Hard Sudoku

8			2		6		3	7
	9		5				1	
4		7	9		3			
		1	6			7	8	
		6				1		3
			8	5				
6							5	
	7		4	8		6		
	5				9			

Hard Sudoku

1		7		3	4			
					1			5
	6	5					8	
	9			5	8	1	2	
7						6		
4	5				3		9	7
	3			7			4	2
8	7		4					
		6		1				

36

Hard Sudoku

5		7	4		8		2	3
	2	8		7		1	4	
				3		5		
		9	7		1	3	8	2
		5	9					7
		2						
						7	9	
4		1	6			2		
7		3		9				4

Hard Sudoku

5		7		3		8		
9		3			6	2		4
	6		7	1				5
		2			7			8
8	4	9				5		
1							9	
	5					4		3
				7		6		9
3				8	4			

Hard Sudoku

3		2		1		7	5	
	5				3		1	
		1	8					4
			9		2		8	
5						9		7
8	2			4				
		6	4	8	1	2		5
	3	5				8		6

Hard Sudoku

4					6	2	5	
	5						8	1
	7	8				4	6	
	2			9			1	5
			6	2		9		
		4	8	3	5			6
			9	6		1	4	
8			1	4				2
	4	7						

Hard Sudoku

1			4		8	9		
5				6			4	2
7	8		2	9				6
		3	9					
2	5							
		7	1		2	3	6	8
				1			8	4
6	9							1
		8				5		

41

Hard Sudoku

8	3	7	4				5	2
5	4		2					
1		2					7	
	9			1	2	8		4
	8		6					5
				4		9		3
		4		2	7			
9			8	6				
3	7							

Hard Sudoku

1	2						5	8
			7			1		
6	3		1					4
2				6	7		9	
3		1			9			5
8					3			
				3		7	6	2
							4	
9	5							

Hard Sudoku

1		3			8			9
	5		9	6				8
6			1		5	7		
		6	5	2			4	
7					4			5
	4							1
		1	2		3			
	3				9	8		
9	7							

Hard Sudoku

6		7						
9				3		4	2	8
8				5			6	
					2			6
	7	9	6			8		
2		8						5
			5		4	6		7
	5		1	9				3
		1	2				9	

Hard Sudoku

4			3	6	7			9
6	2			4		7		3
	1					6		
8	6		9			1		
		7						2
		2		7				8
3		1						
	8	4	2		6	9		
					1			4

Hard Sudoku

8						2		
1	2	4			8			6
	6			4		7		
				9		4	1	
			7					2
	4	5						7
			3	8	9	6		4
		3	5					8
7	8				1	9		5

Hard Sudoku

5		7	3	2	9			
		1				2	3	6
			1	3			6	5
1	4		7	5		9	2	
3						4		
	8		5			6	1	
				4				
7			6		3	5		8

Hard Sudoku

<table>
<tr><td>4</td><td>2</td><td>6</td><td></td><td></td><td>7</td><td></td><td>5</td><td>8</td></tr>
<tr><td></td><td>3</td><td></td><td></td><td>8</td><td></td><td>7</td><td></td><td>6</td></tr>
<tr><td>1</td><td></td><td>7</td><td></td><td></td><td></td><td></td><td></td><td>2</td></tr>
<tr><td></td><td>1</td><td></td><td>6</td><td></td><td></td><td>8</td><td></td><td>9</td></tr>
<tr><td>9</td><td>6</td><td></td><td></td><td>1</td><td>2</td><td></td><td></td><td></td></tr>
<tr><td></td><td></td><td></td><td></td><td></td><td></td><td></td><td>4</td><td>1</td></tr>
<tr><td></td><td></td><td>1</td><td></td><td>2</td><td></td><td></td><td></td><td>5</td></tr>
<tr><td></td><td></td><td></td><td>5</td><td></td><td>8</td><td></td><td>6</td><td>3</td></tr>
<tr><td></td><td>5</td><td></td><td></td><td></td><td></td><td></td><td></td><td></td></tr>
</table>

Hard Sudoku

8		5		3	6		4	
		2				5		1
					2			6
				4	3			
9	5		2			3		
4							6	2
					4	7		
				5				9
2	3	6	1				8	

Hard Sudoku

4		1				6		
	3				6	7		
	5		7	9				
			6	3		5	1	
	9		8	1				
		3		7		2		
5	1	4						
		2				3	4	
		7	4				8	

Kakuro

■	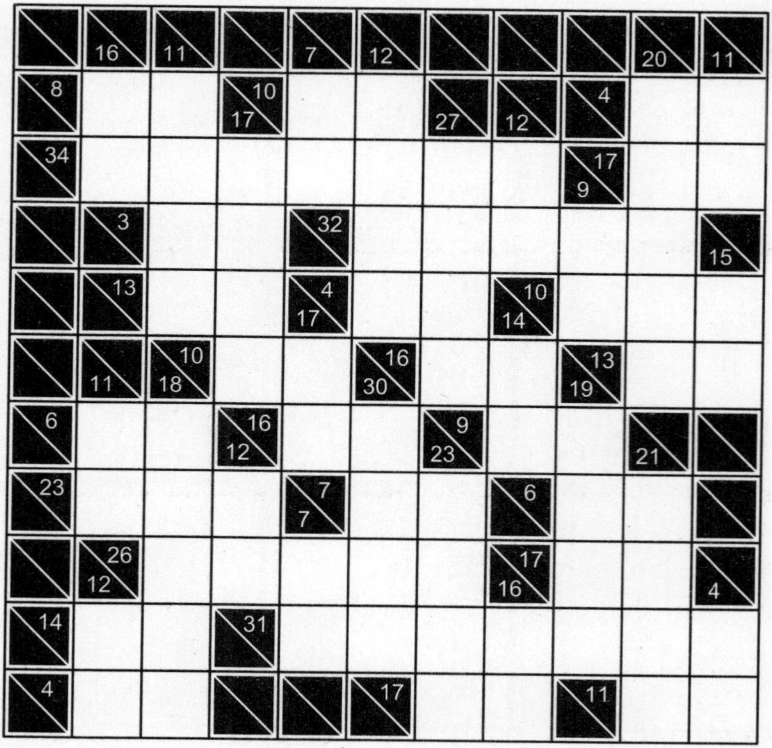 16\	11\	■	7\	12\	■	■	■	20\	11\
\8			17\10			27\	12\	\4		
\34								9\17		
■	\3			\32						15\
■	\13			17\4			14\10			
■	11\	18\10			30\16			19\13		
\6			12\16			23\9			21\	■
\23				7\7			\6			■
■	12\26						16\17			4\
\14			\31							
\4			■	■	\17			\11		

Kakuro

■	24\	31\	7\	24\	■	15\	8\	■	12\	20\
\26					\6			\4		
\13					20\16			5\12		
\17			13\8				17\20			
■	4\25					10\9			23\	16\
\7				4\19				11\14		
\12			11\14				23\10			
■	19\	12\3			24\24					17\
\13				17\21				13\3		
\14			\16			\16				
\13			\17			\28				

Kakuro

■	16\	17\	■	■	■	11\	8\	■	■	■
\17			28\	13\	\3			6\	38\	10\
\29					14\24					
■	13\	28\24				5\	11\18			
\19				\23						6\
\9				6\	11\3			20\12		
\11			24\3			17\	\9			
■	7\35						10\19			
\12				4\	12\23				4\	13\
\31						\11				
■	■	■	\6			■	■	\11		

Kakuro

■	■	■	↓23	↓17	■	■	■	↓16	↓13	↓4
■	↓12	→9 ↓7			↓10	↓35	→7			
→27							→13 ↓4			
→23				→26 ↓17					↓6	↓23
■	↓8	→16 ↓12			→24 ↓19					
→3			→20				↓8	→7		
→9			↓20	→16 ↓13				→10 ↓16		
→21						→16 ↓16			↓17	↓12
■	↓17	→14 ↓4					→21 ↓4			
→18				→31						
→19				■	■	→3			■	■

Kakuro

■	■	■	11\	17\	■	32\	16\	4\	■	■
■	20\	19\9			\15				16\	10\
\16					9\23					
\21				14\16			19\	24\17		
\9			16\19						18\	■
■	\20				30\28					■
■	\11					4\11				22\
■	11\	17\31						23\10		
\16			5\	12\11			8\24			
\31						\15				
■	■	\8				\16			■	■

Kakuro

■	■	■	10\	6\	■	12\	27\	14\	■	■
■	17\	12\4			\7				7\	■
\17					6\24					16\
\4			\4			12\26				
\15			12\	\11				9\8		
■	\10			23\	10\22				30\	■
■	3\	12\7				17\	\12			11\
\11			20\23				7\	\8		
\17					5\9			10\15		
■	\22					\23				
■	■	\6				\3			■	■

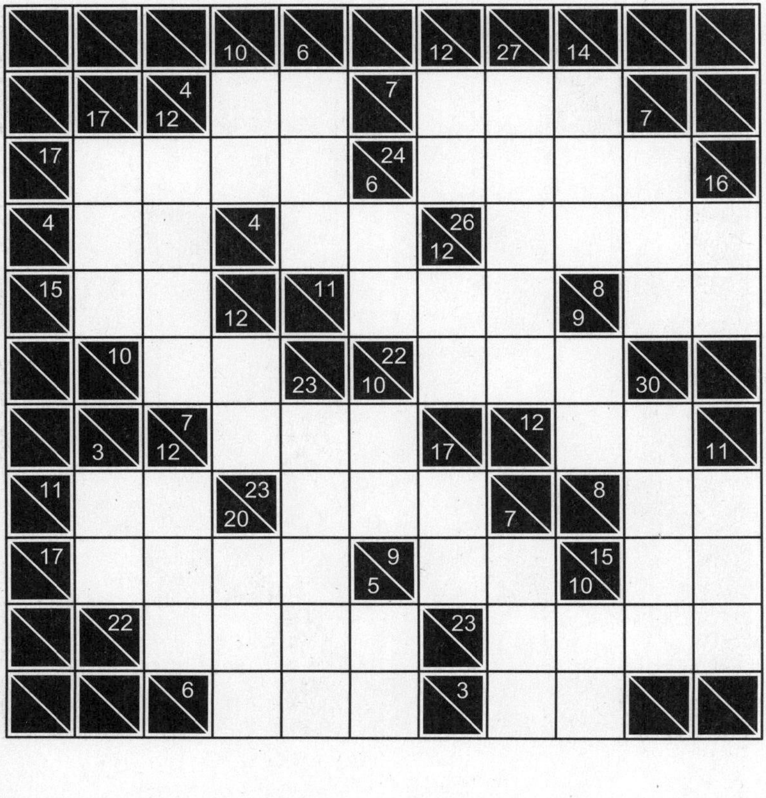

Kakuro

■	■	■	13\	4\	■	■	■	16\	22\	■
■	7\	12\11			16\	13\	\8			16\
\30							11\19			
\4			25\	6\10				28\14		
■	3\	36\19				\19				12\
\20						15\	16\15			
\17				11\	\28					
■	3\17				15\24				9\	13\
\4			14\10				16\	8\16		
\16				\29						
■	\16			■	■	\14			■	■

Kakuro

■	4\	15\	■	■	7\	4\	8\	■	■	■
\11			26\	\7				9\	37\	■
\16				24\19						■
■	20\	25\6				6\	26\17			27\
\27					\4			\12		
\30					17\12			12\14		
\4			\16			\23				
\3			3\11			12\10				
■	\4			12\	4\21				8\	13\
■	\19						\10			
■	■	■	\7				■	\16		

Kakuro

■	14\	8\	■	■	14\	15\	■	10\	32\	■
\8			11\	\16			20\10			■
\20				16\20						16\
■	16\	35\14			28\	15\22				
\11			3\30					3\8		
\11				\12			\11			3\
■	16\3			18\9			7\9			
\17			13\17					13\8		
\28					17\	9\10			13\	8\
■	\27						\12			
■	\15			\9			■	\16		

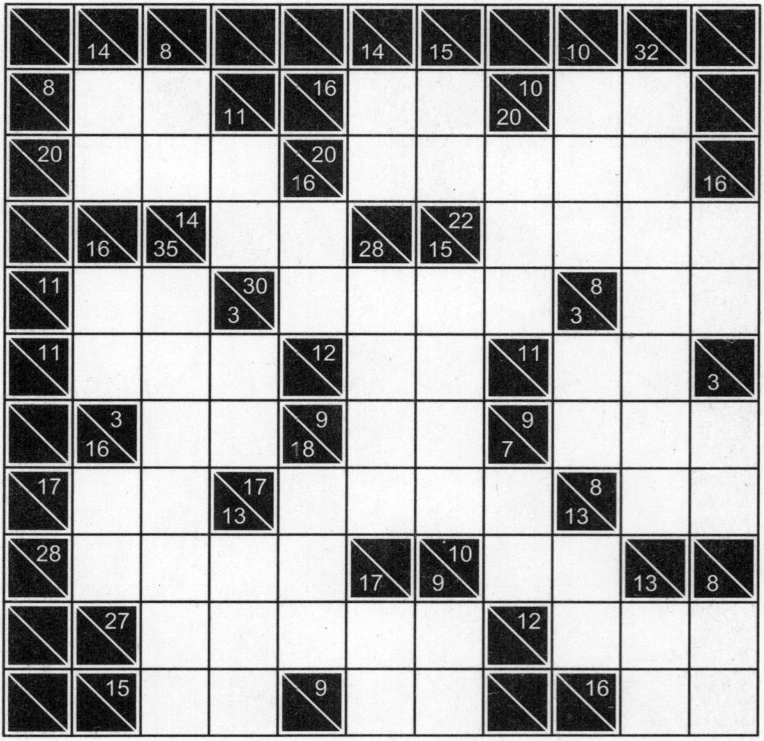

Kakuro

■	■	12\	4\	■	11\	16\	■	14\	29\
■	17\5			\14			15\10		
\13				26\23					
\9			20\8			24\22			
■	\21				\20				
■	23\	29\4			\9			22\	■
\29					7\16				17\
\16				17\3			4\16		
\26						\16			
\15			\9			\3			■

Kakuro

■	■	22\	12\	29\	■	■	■	20\	30\
■	11\6				7\	7\	\9		
\27							8\14		
\4			\26						
\17			24\12			17\21			
■	19\	25\17			23\4			13\	20\
\10				9\16			\4		
\34							16\16		
\17			\34						
\13			■	■	\11				■

12

Kakuro

■	■	31\	8\	■	■	■	■	7\	24\
■	3\16			9\	8\	15\	\8		
\24							16\11		
\4			20\25						
■	\16			\19				27\	■
■	\5			18\	13\	\4			■
■	18\	11\14				3\8			9\
\32							12\16		
\3			\27						
\16			■	■	■	\4			■

Kakuro

\	\	28\	11\	7\	\	5\	32\	30\	\
\	14\20				\16				\
\19					12\9				3\
\16			36\4			4\17			
\	\5			4\27					
\	17\	20\12			11\11			15\	\
\31						11\10			4\
\24				6\4			14\3		
\	\15				\11				
\	\8				\22				\

Kakuro

■	4\	27\	■	16\	22\	■	■	6\	7\
\6			4\8			22\	\6		
\27							23\4		
■	4\12			32\16					
\3			10\26					26\	11\
\22					20\28				
■	23\	12\28					8\4		
\26						16\16			4\
\16			\25						
\7			■	\14			\3		

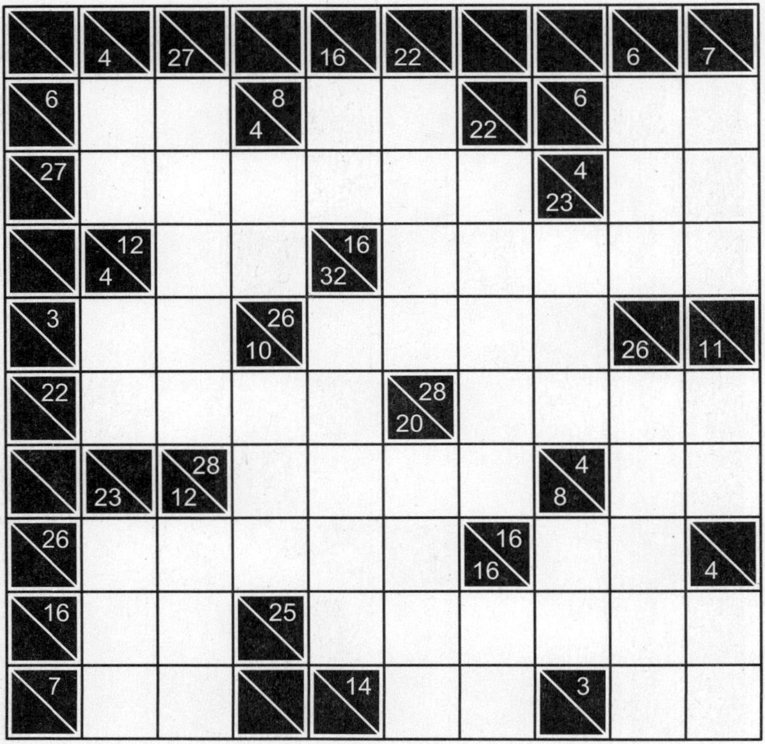

15

Kakuro

■	14\	16\	■	■	7\	16\	■	30\	9\
\16			3\	\9			16\16		
\12				27\24					
■	\12				8\	21\11			6\
■	17\	21\	\36						
\9			18\12				\4		
\38							5\	23\	■
■	17\5			16\	11\12				9\
\31						\14			
\16			\17			■	\16		

Kakuro

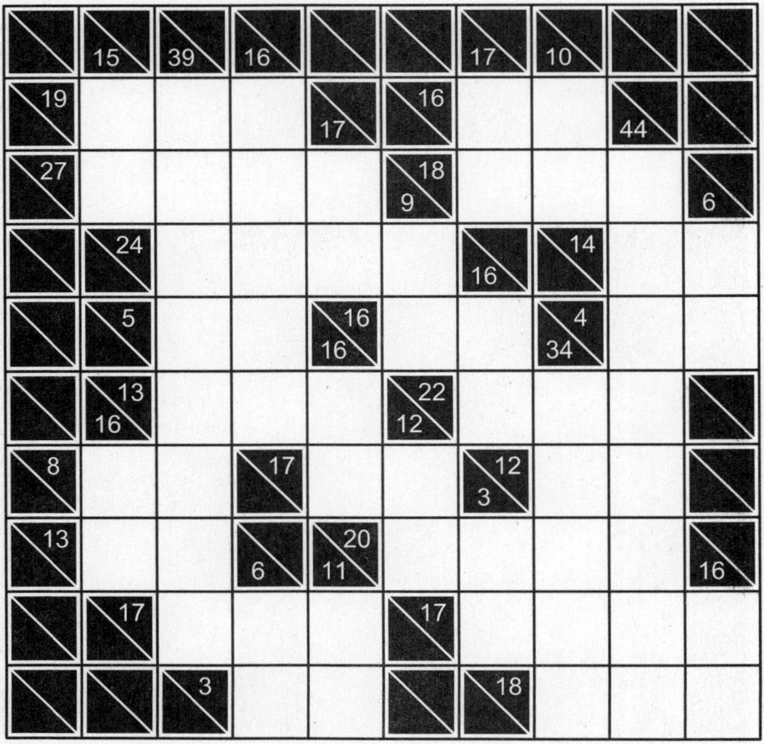

■	↓15	↓39	↓16	■	■	↓17	↓10	■	■
→19				↓17	→16			↓44	■
→27					↓9 →18				↓6
■	→24					↓16	→14		
■	→5			↓16 →16			↓34 →4		
■	↓16 →13				↓12 →22				■
→8			→17			↓3 →12			■
→13			↓6	↓11 →20					↓16
■	→17				→17				
■	■	→3			■	→18			

Kakuro

■	■	■	14 \	7 \	18 \	■	10 \	25 \	■
■	16 \	15 \ 12				10 \ 4			■
\ 41									9 \
\ 8			18 \ 14				13 \ 16		
■	\ 16			18 \ 28					
■	11 \	24 \ 10			10 \ 4			10 \	■
\ 24						9 \ 3			11 \
\ 3			9 \ 18				17 \ 3		
■	\ 41								
■	\ 17			\ 12				■	■

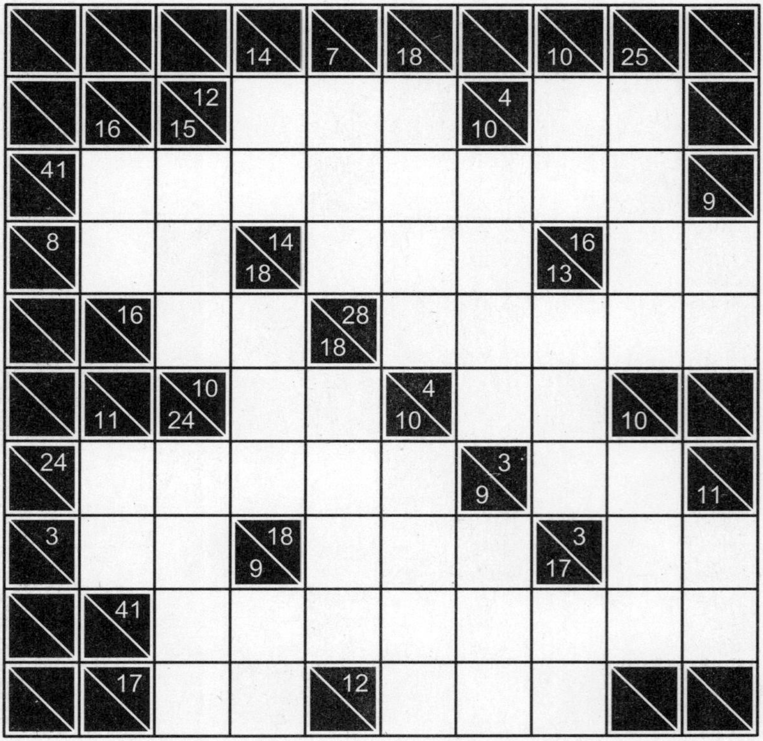

18

Kakuro

■	■	16\	18\	■	■	9\	6\	28\	■
■	\3			25\	\12				7\
■	12\24				3\10				
\36							9\13		
\4			12\11			20\11			
■	7\	15\4			11\17			29\	16\
\21				19\4			11\17		
\6			14\28						
\20					\23				■
■	\14				■	\9			■

Kakuro

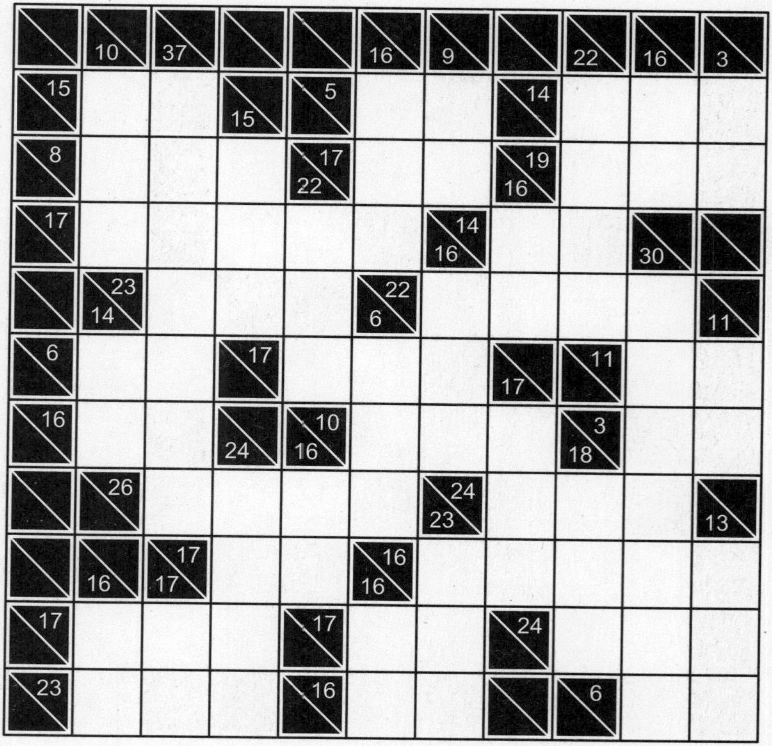

\	10\	37\	\	\	16\	9\	\	22\	16\	3\
\15			15\	\5			\14			
\8				22\17			16\19			
\17						16\14			30\	\
\	14\23				6\22					11\
\6			\17				17\	\11		
\16			24\	16\10				18\3		
\	\26					23\24				13\
\	16\	17\17			16\16					
\17				\17			\24			
\23				\16			\	\6		

Kakuro

■	↓13	↓4	■	■	↓11	↓17	■	■	↓35	↓9
→11			↓11	↓19 →17			↓12	→6		
→39								→11		
■	↓3	↓35 →3			↓8 →4			↓4 →12		
→22						↓22	→3			■
→11			↓17	→11			→7			↓16
■	→11			→9			↓11	↓18 →10		
■	↓15 →15			↓14	↓20 →33					
→3			→16			↓9 →3			↓16	↓5
→17			→35							
→9			■	→17			■	→9		

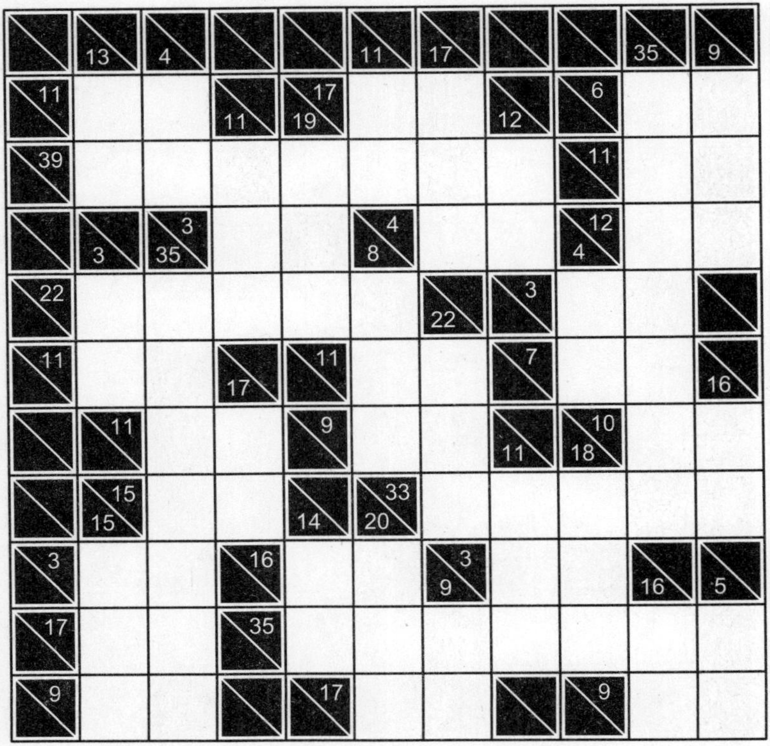

21

Kakuro

■	7\	10\	16\	■	■	3\	12\	■	■
\23				20\	\11			23\	7\
\19					7\11				
■	4\	20\	\11			30\	16\10		
\3			11\22						14\
\12					9\18				
■	14\21						\16		
\10			17\	16\17			17\	6\	4\
\29					\23				
■	■	\16			■	\11			

Kakuro

■	■ ↓12	■ ↓11	■	■ ↓4	■ ↓12	■	■ ↓17	■ ↓21	■
■ →10			■ ↓24 →12			■ ↓23 →9			■
■ →39									■ ↓9
■ →7				■ →4			■ ↓25 →16		
■	■ →3			■ ↓14	■ →10				
■	■ ↓3	■ ↓30 →8			■ →13			■ ↓16	■
■ →17					■ ↓8	■ →4			■ ↓12
■ →11			■ ↓11 →12			■ ↓4 →13			
■	■ →36								
■	■ →17			■ →3			■ →12		

Kakuro

■	■	■	↓5	↓6	■	↓23	↓16	↓15	■
■	↓6	↓28 →4			→14				↓16
→16					↓11 →29				
→12			↓15	↓28 →3			↓13 →17		
→39								↓28	■
■	→7				↓4 →21				↓15
■	↓11	↓16 →33							
→3			↓17 →3			↓9	↓17 →10		
→29					→30				
■	→20				→9			■	■

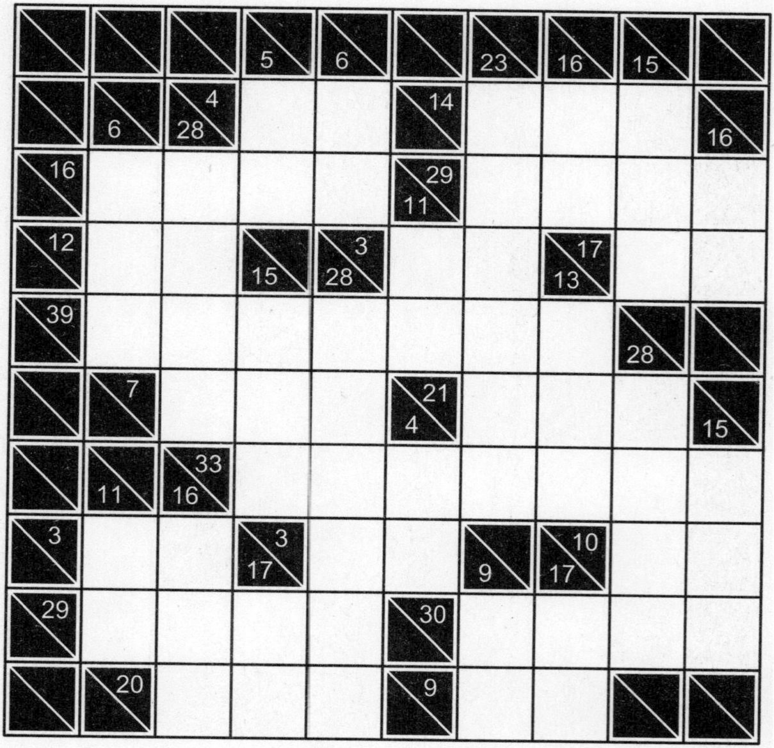

Kakuro

\	\	11\	17\	\	\	3\	26\	\	\
\	\12			12\	\11			7\	\
\	8\11				24\8				15\
\3			\11			\10			
\11			29\14			24\21			
\	16\	10\22						18\	9\
\18				\8			\6		
\24				3\3			9\17		
\	\6				\14				\
\	\	\5			\	\6			\

Kakuro

■	■	20\	8\	9\	■	17\	16\	■	■
■	22\7				\17			24\	8\
\25					4\28				
\7			13\6			6\	10\12		
\22				10\18					
■	21\	13\3			14\4			11\	15\
\31						19\12			
\14			13\	4\16			4\3		
\12					\25				
■	■	\12			\7				■

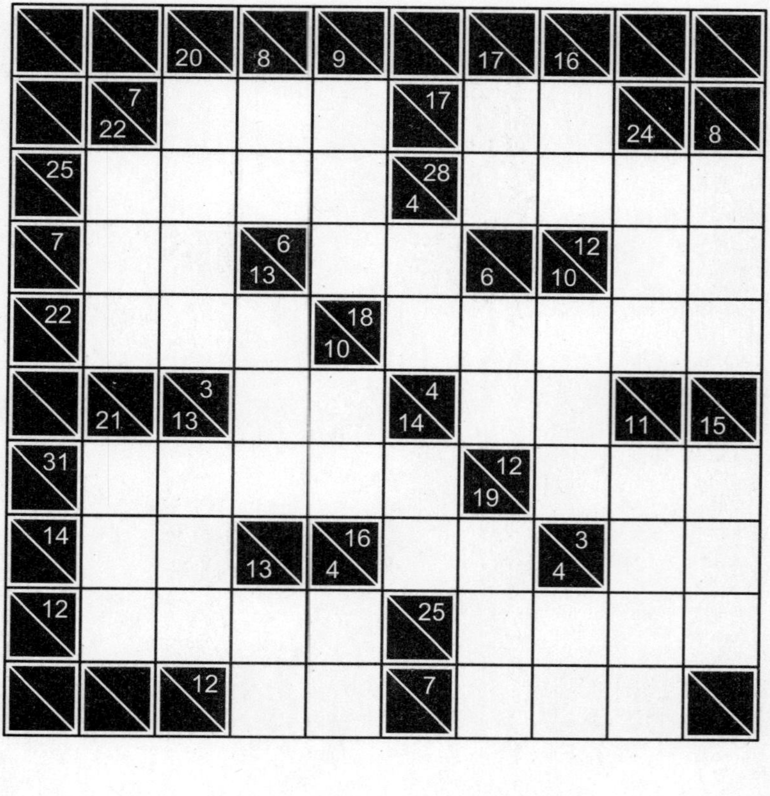

Kakuro

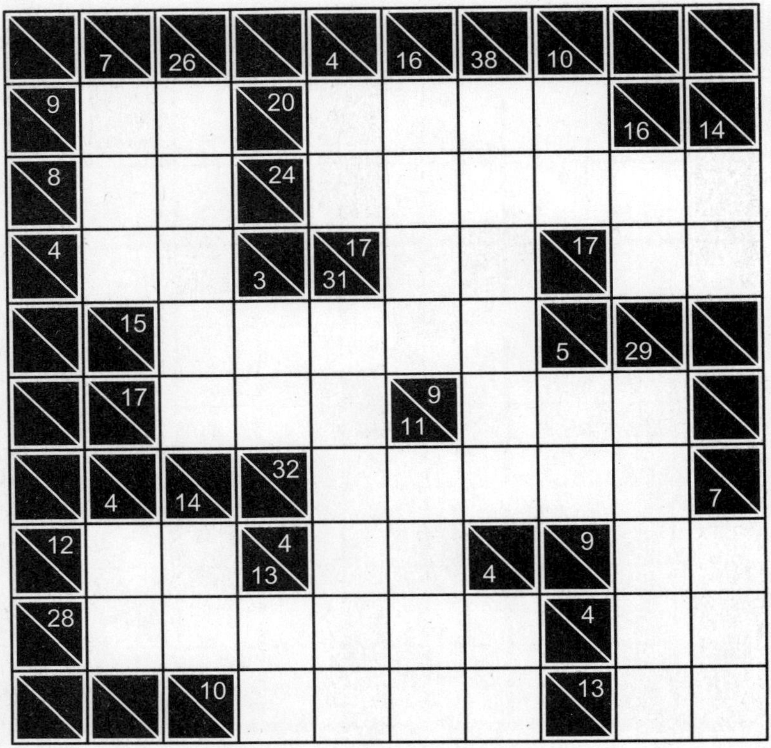

■	↓7	↓26	■	↓4	↓16	↓38	↓10	■	■
→9			→20					↓16	↓14
→8			→24						
→4			↓3	↓31 →17			→17		
■	→15						↓5	↓29	■
■	→17				↓11 →9				■
■	↓4	↓14	→32						↓7
→12			↓13 →4			↓4	→9		
→28							→4		
■	■	→10					→13		

Godoku

H	F				C			
I	E				B	C	A	
		A			D	G		
		I	B	A			E	C
D				F				A
B	A			C	H	I		
		F	H			A		
	C	H	I				G	D
			C				H	I

Godoku

	B	H			I			D
D	I							
			H	D	B		A	C
	A		B				D	H
E		G	I		D	C		F
B	F				C		I	
H	G		D	I	F			
							G	E
A			G			D	F	

Godoku

F		B			I	H		A
					H			
E		A	F	C		G		I
B	F					C		
		H		F		E		
		C					G	F
H		I		G	F	D		B
			E					
D		F	B			I		G

Godoku

C		D			B	A		E
					E			
B		E	I	D		F		G
E	C					I		
		A		E		B		
		B					E	F
D		F		B	I	H		C
			H					
A		H	F			G		I

Godoku

A	H			I	F			B
	D		G				H	F
		G				D		
B				D			C	
G			I	H	C			E
	I			A				D
		F				H		
D	C				B		F	
H			E	F			I	C

Godoku

			D	G		I		
		D	F		C	E		B
				I		C		
		I		E		B		A
B			I	C	D			G
E		F		B		D		
		G		D				
I		B	E		H	G		
		E		F	I			

Godoku

C		D		F	I			A
F	A							
		B	C	D		H		
		C	I	G		A		E
	B	I				F	G	
H		A		E	D	I		
		F		I	G	E		
							D	B
A			H	B		G		F

Godoku

		B	E				I	
A				F	H	E		
	G	H	I			C		A
	D					H		F
	B						D	
G		F					C	
H		C			A	G	B	
		G	H	B				C
	E				F	A		

Godoku

B	C		G				A	E
	E	F			A		D	
G			H				C	
	G	C	A	B				
D								A
				E	D	C	G	
	F				C			B
	D		E			I	F	
E	I				F		H	C

Godoku

	G				E	I	H	
I					B	C		A
A	F	D			H	B		
F	C	I		G				
			E		F			
				H		G	F	C
		F	D			A	C	B
E		G	F					D
	D	C	H				E	

Godoku

G						B	A	F
A		D			E	C		
F	I			G			E	
	F		C		D			
		H		I		D		
			E		B		H	
	D			B			F	H
		F	D			G		A
B	G	A						C

Godoku

		C	H	B			I	
A				G	C			
					E			C
	A	B	C		G			I
I	F			A			E	D
H			E		I	A	G	
D			F					
			I	E				G
	B			C	D	I		

Godoku

	B	C					F	G
G				H				D
A	D		F				I	
		A		D	C		H	
C		B		F		I		A
	H		E	A		G		
	C				F		B	H
D				E				F
B	F					E	A	

Godoku

		D		I	C	A		
	C		D				E	
H				A	G			C
F		I					H	
E		H		C		G		A
	A					I		B
I			A	F				G
	G				B		A	
		B	C	G		H		

Godoku

	H	G						A
D	I		A	B				G
		C		G				D
	B		F		D		H	
C			E	I	G			F
	G		B		A		D	
G				A		F		
H				D	B		E	C
E						D	G	

Godoku

G		E	I		C		H	B
B				E		G		
	H		A					D
A			H		E	D		C
	E						A	
H		D	F		G			I
C					I		G	
		B		H				A
D	G		C		A	F		E

Godoku

D		I			C		H	G
		G	D	H				
F			G		E	B	D	
		H					B	C
			H		B			
A	I					H		
	C	A	E		F			B
				B	D	G		
G	B		I			F		E

Godoku

	H			F	B			E
			C			D		
B	A	E						
E	C		B	H	F	I		
	I	A		E		B	G	
		B	A	I	G		E	F
						H	A	C
		C			A			
A			F	C			B	

Godoku

			D	G	E			
	I		F		C		G	
		H				C		
D	G						C	A
B	H		I	C	D		E	G
E	C						H	I
		G				A		
	D		E		H		C	
			G	F	I			

Godoku

				I	D		C	
B		G				I		
	F	I	H	B		E	A	
F				C		A		
E		C	D		H	F		I
		B		A				C
	B	E		H	I	C	F	
		F				G		H
	I		A	F				

Godoku

		A	B				G	
C	I				H		A	
				A	F			D
	C	B		D				H
		H	A	B	I	G		
I				E		F	D	
H			C	I				
	D		G				H	E
	E				B	C		

Godoku

A	B	I			F			E
				G	A	C		B
	G	F		H		I		D
B	H							
	F	D				A	E	
							G	H
F		E		C		H	B	
H		G	D	E				
I			G			E	D	C

Godoku

H			D			A		G
	I					B	E	
A	D	E	F			H		
			B	D	C	F		E
			G		H			
F		D	E	A	I			
		I			F	D	B	H
	A	H					G	
B		G			D			I

Godoku

F			D	E	I			A
	I				H		F	
		A		C		G		
B	F			D				H
G		H	I		C	E		D
I				B			G	F
		I		G		D		
	B		E				H	
D			B	H	A			G

Godoku

G			H				I	A
A		H		G		E		F
B						G		
	A			D				I
	F	G		A		C	E	
H				F			G	
		I						E
C		A		E		F		G
F	B				D			H

8	4	3	9	2	6	1	5	7
5	9	6	3	7	1	8	2	4
1	2	7	8	5	4	6	9	3
3	5	4	1	6	8	9	7	2
7	6	1	5	9	2	3	4	8
9	8	2	4	3	7	5	1	6
2	7	8	6	1	5	4	3	9
4	1	9	2	8	3	7	6	5
6	3	5	7	4	9	2	8	1

Easy Sudoku 1

5	4	1	7	8	9	3	6	2
3	8	2	1	5	6	7	4	9
6	7	9	2	3	4	5	8	1
2	9	3	5	1	8	4	7	6
7	5	6	9	4	2	8	1	3
8	1	4	6	7	3	9	2	5
9	6	8	3	2	7	1	5	4
4	3	5	8	6	1	2	9	7
1	2	7	4	9	5	6	3	8

Easy Sudoku 2

5	2	3	8	6	1	9	7	4
4	6	8	9	2	7	1	5	3
9	1	7	3	4	5	6	2	8
3	5	9	4	8	6	7	1	2
6	4	1	7	5	2	3	8	9
7	8	2	1	3	9	4	6	5
1	3	4	2	7	8	5	9	6
8	9	5	6	1	4	2	3	7
2	7	6	5	9	3	8	4	1

Easy Sudoku 3

4	2	7	6	9	8	5	1	3
3	8	9	1	4	5	7	6	2
1	5	6	2	7	3	4	8	9
9	1	4	3	2	6	8	7	5
5	3	2	4	8	7	6	9	1
6	7	8	5	1	9	2	3	4
7	9	1	8	5	2	3	4	6
2	4	3	7	6	1	9	5	8
8	6	5	9	3	4	1	2	7

Easy Sudoku 4

1	2	5	8	3	6	9	4	7
3	6	8	4	7	9	2	5	1
7	9	4	5	1	2	6	8	3
2	8	6	9	4	7	1	3	5
4	1	3	6	5	8	7	9	2
9	5	7	3	2	1	8	6	4
5	7	9	1	6	4	3	2	8
6	3	1	2	8	5	4	7	9
8	4	2	7	9	3	5	1	6

Easy Sudoku 5

4	5	6	1	2	8	7	3	9
7	8	2	9	4	3	1	5	6
3	9	1	5	6	7	2	4	8
5	7	3	4	9	6	8	2	1
6	1	4	7	8	2	3	9	5
8	2	9	3	1	5	4	6	7
9	6	7	8	3	4	5	1	2
1	3	8	2	5	9	6	7	4
2	4	5	6	7	1	9	8	3

Easy Sudoku 6

6	9	8	7	5	4	2	1	3
1	2	7	6	9	3	8	4	5
3	4	5	1	2	8	7	6	9
9	5	2	8	6	7	1	3	4
8	6	1	3	4	9	5	7	2
7	3	4	5	1	2	6	9	8
4	7	9	2	8	6	3	5	1
5	8	6	9	3	1	4	2	7
2	1	3	4	7	5	9	8	6

Easy Sudoku 7

7	5	3	2	1	6	4	9	8
6	1	4	9	3	8	7	5	2
8	2	9	4	5	7	6	1	3
4	7	1	5	2	3	8	6	9
2	8	5	6	7	9	3	4	1
9	3	6	8	4	1	2	7	5
5	4	7	3	9	2	1	8	6
3	9	8	1	6	4	5	2	7
1	6	2	7	8	5	9	3	4

Easy Sudoku 8

5	8	2	6	9	3	7	1	4
9	3	6	1	4	7	2	5	8
1	4	7	8	5	2	6	9	3
6	9	5	2	7	8	4	3	1
7	1	4	3	6	5	9	8	2
3	2	8	4	1	9	5	6	7
8	5	3	9	2	4	1	7	6
2	7	1	5	3	6	8	4	9
4	6	9	7	8	1	3	2	5

Easy Sudoku 9

1	7	8	2	6	9	4	5	3
6	2	9	3	4	5	7	8	1
5	3	4	7	8	1	9	6	2
2	1	5	6	7	8	3	4	9
7	8	3	5	9	4	2	1	6
4	9	6	1	2	3	5	7	8
8	5	7	9	3	6	1	2	4
9	4	2	8	1	7	6	3	5
3	6	1	4	5	2	8	9	7

Easy Sudoku 10

4	9	6	3	1	7	5	2	8
7	8	3	4	2	5	9	1	6
1	2	5	6	8	9	7	3	4
2	3	8	5	9	1	6	4	7
6	1	9	7	3	4	8	5	2
5	7	4	2	6	8	1	9	3
8	4	7	9	5	3	2	6	1
3	5	2	1	7	6	4	8	9
9	6	1	8	4	2	3	7	5

Easy Sudoku 11

9	4	6	7	5	2	1	8	3
5	3	7	8	4	1	2	6	9
8	1	2	6	9	3	7	4	5
1	7	8	4	6	5	3	9	2
3	2	5	9	1	8	4	7	6
4	6	9	2	3	7	5	1	8
6	5	4	1	2	9	8	3	7
7	9	3	5	8	4	6	2	1
2	8	1	3	7	6	9	5	4

Easy Sudoku 12

[illegible]	6	3	8	9	7	5	1	2
[illegible]	7	9	1	2	3	6	8	4
[illegible]	1	2	4	5	6	7	9	3
[illegible]	9	5	3	4	2	1	7	8
[illegible]	3	1	9	6	8	2	4	5
[illegible]	4	8	5	7	1	9	3	6
[illegible]	5	7	2	3	4	8	6	1
[illegible]	2	4	6	8	9	3	5	7
[illegible]	8	6	7	1	5	4	2	9

Easy Sudoku 13

1	7	5	2	3	4	6	8	9
3	6	8	5	7	9	1	2	4
4	9	2	8	1	6	5	3	7
5	8	1	9	4	3	2	7	6
7	2	4	1	6	5	8	9	3
6	3	9	7	8	2	4	1	5
8	4	6	3	2	7	9	5	1
9	1	7	4	5	8	3	6	2
2	5	3	6	9	1	7	4	8

Easy Sudoku 14

4	5	2	3	6	7	1	9	8
6	7	9	2	8	1	3	4	5
8	1	3	9	4	5	6	2	7
1	3	4	5	2	8	7	6	9
5	2	6	4	7	9	8	1	3
7	9	8	6	1	3	2	5	4
9	6	5	7	3	2	4	8	1
2	8	7	1	5	4	9	3	6
3	4	1	8	9	6	5	7	2

Easy Sudoku 15

1	5	3	9	6	7	4	2	8
8	9	6	1	2	4	3	5	7
2	7	4	3	8	5	9	6	1
6	1	2	8	7	9	5	4	3
9	8	5	6	4	3	7	1	2
3	4	7	2	5	1	6	8	9
7	2	1	4	9	6	8	3	5
4	3	9	5	1	8	2	7	6
5	6	8	7	3	2	1	9	4

Easy Sudoku 16

3	8	1	7	5	2	4	9	6
5	9	6	1	3	4	7	2	8
2	4	7	6	8	9	1	3	5
8	6	9	2	4	7	3	5	1
7	1	5	3	9	6	8	4	2
4	3	2	5	1	8	6	7	9
9	7	8	4	2	1	5	6	3
6	2	3	8	7	5	9	1	4
1	5	4	9	6	3	2	8	7

Easy Sudoku 17

6	3	8	1	4	5	7	2	9
5	9	7	2	3	8	6	1	4
1	2	4	9	6	7	5	3	8
4	5	9	3	7	1	8	6	2
3	6	1	4	8	2	9	5	7
7	8	2	5	9	6	1	4	3
8	7	5	6	2	4	3	9	1
9	4	6	7	1	3	2	8	5
2	1	3	8	5	9	4	7	6

Easy Sudoku 18

9	4	7	5	3	6	8	2	1
2	1	6	7	4	8	3	5	9
5	3	8	9	2	1	4	6	7
1	6	9	8	7	2	5	3	4
7	5	3	6	9	4	2	1	8
4	8	2	1	5	3	7	9	6
3	9	5	4	1	7	6	8	2
6	7	1	2	8	5	9	4	3
8	2	4	3	6	9	1	7	5

Easy Sudoku 19

4	2	3	7	5	6	9	8	
5	7	1	3	8	9	2	4	
6	8	9	1	4	2	5	3	
7	6	8	4	9	1	3	5	
9	1	5	8	2	3	6	7	
2	3	4	5	6	7	8	1	
1	5	6	9	7	8	4	2	
8	9	7	2	3	4	1	6	
3	4	2	6	1	5	7	9	

Easy Sudoku 20

1	6	5	3	8	2	7	9	4
2	7	4	9	1	6	3	5	8
8	9	3	7	4	5	1	6	2
3	2	8	5	7	4	6	1	9
9	4	7	6	3	1	8	2	5
5	1	6	8	2	9	4	7	3
6	3	2	1	5	8	9	4	7
4	8	9	2	6	7	5	3	1
7	5	1	4	9	3	2	8	6

Easy Sudoku 21

4	8	9	6	5	1	7	2	3
6	1	2	7	9	3	8	5	4
3	5	7	4	8	2	9	1	6
7	9	3	5	4	8	2	6	1
1	6	5	2	7	9	3	4	8
8	2	4	3	1	6	5	9	7
5	3	6	1	2	7	4	8	9
9	4	1	8	3	5	6	7	2
2	7	8	9	6	4	1	3	5

Easy Sudoku 22

7	8	1	2	4	3	5	9	6
5	9	2	6	1	7	3	8	4
6	3	4	5	8	9	1	7	2
8	2	6	7	5	4	9	3	1
9	7	3	8	2	1	6	4	5
4	1	5	9	3	6	7	2	8
2	4	9	1	7	5	8	6	3
3	5	7	4	6	8	2	1	9
1	6	8	3	9	2	4	5	7

Easy Sudoku 23

2	8	4	7	5	1	9	3	6
3	5	7	8	9	6	4	2	1
6	9	1	2	3	4	7	5	8
9	2	3	1	4	5	8	6	7
1	4	8	3	6	7	5	9	2
5	7	6	9	8	2	1	4	3
4	6	2	5	7	8	3	1	9
7	1	9	4	2	3	6	8	5
8	3	5	6	1	9	2	7	4

Easy Sudoku 24

[illegible]	6	4	9	1	5	3	2	7
[illegible]	9	1	6	2	3	5	8	4
2	3	5	4	7	8	1	6	9
[illegible]	4	6	5	8	1	7	3	2
[illegible]	2	3	7	6	9	4	5	8
5	7	8	2	3	4	6	9	1
4	1	2	8	5	6	9	7	3
6	8	9	3	4	7	2	1	5
3	5	7	1	9	2	8	4	6

Easy Sudoku 25

2	4	7	5	9	3	6	1	8
1	3	6	4	7	8	5	2	9
9	8	5	1	2	6	3	4	7
3	2	9	6	8	1	7	5	4
4	5	1	7	3	2	8	9	6
6	7	8	9	4	5	1	3	2
8	6	3	2	1	9	4	7	5
5	9	4	3	6	7	2	8	1
7	1	2	8	5	4	9	6	3

Easy Sudoku 26

1	2	6	3	9	5	8	4	7
8	9	5	7	2	4	6	1	3
7	3	4	6	1	8	9	5	2
4	1	2	5	8	3	7	6	9
3	5	7	4	6	9	2	8	1
6	8	9	2	7	1	4	3	5
2	6	3	8	5	7	1	9	4
9	4	8	1	3	2	5	7	6
5	7	1	9	4	6	3	2	8

Easy Sudoku 27

5	3	8	4	2	1	7	6	9
6	4	9	7	5	3	2	8	1
1	7	2	6	8	9	3	4	5
7	2	5	1	3	8	4	9	6
3	9	4	2	6	5	8	1	7
8	6	1	9	7	4	5	2	3
9	5	6	8	4	7	1	3	2
4	1	7	3	9	2	6	5	8
2	8	3	5	1	6	9	7	4

Easy Sudoku 28

5	6	8	4	7	9	1	2	3
7	9	2	3	5	1	4	8	6
1	3	4	6	2	8	9	7	5
3	7	6	8	9	2	5	1	4
8	4	1	5	3	7	6	9	2
9	2	5	1	6	4	8	3	7
6	5	9	7	8	3	2	4	1
2	1	3	9	4	6	7	5	8
4	8	7	2	1	5	3	6	9

Easy Sudoku 29

9	3	2	1	4	6	8	5	7
1	4	5	2	8	7	9	6	3
6	8	7	3	5	9	1	2	4
2	5	9	6	7	4	3	8	1
4	6	3	8	1	5	2	7	9
7	1	8	9	2	3	5	4	6
3	2	1	4	6	8	7	9	5
8	7	6	5	9	1	4	3	2
5	9	4	7	3	2	6	1	8

Easy Sudoku 30

3	2	6	7	4	1	8	9	5
1	5	8	6	2	9	4	3	7
4	7	9	3	8	5	1	2	6
5	3	1	8	7	6	2	4	9
6	9	2	5	3	4	7	8	1
7	8	4	9	1	2	5	6	3
8	6	5	4	9	7	3	1	2
9	1	3	2	5	8	6	7	4
2	4	7	1	6	3	9	5	8

Easy Sudoku 31

8	2	3	1	4	5	9	6	7
4	5	9	3	6	7	1	8	2
6	7	1	8	2	9	3	4	5
9	6	7	2	1	8	4	5	3
1	8	5	9	3	4	2	7	6
2	3	4	5	7	6	8	9	1
3	9	6	4	5	2	7	1	8
5	4	2	7	8	1	6	3	9
7	1	8	6	9	3	5	2	4

Easy Sudoku 32

9	7	1	6	8	2	4	5	3
8	2	3	5	7	4	1	9	6
6	4	5	1	3	9	8	2	7
1	6	4	8	2	7	5	3	9
2	3	8	9	4	5	6	7	1
5	9	7	3	6	1	2	8	4
3	8	2	7	1	6	9	4	5
4	1	9	2	5	3	7	6	8
7	5	6	4	9	8	3	1	2

Easy Sudoku 33

9	2	5	1	4	6	8	3	7
3	1	4	5	7	8	9	2	6
6	7	8	3	9	2	4	1	5
7	3	6	9	8	5	2	4	1
4	8	2	6	1	3	5	7	9
1	5	9	7	2	4	3	6	8
2	9	7	4	5	1	6	8	3
8	6	1	2	3	9	7	5	4
5	4	3	8	6	7	1	9	2

Easy Sudoku 34

8	5	9	7	6	1	4	2	3
6	3	7	9	4	2	5	1	8
1	2	4	5	8	3	7	6	9
2	4	1	8	7	9	3	5	6
7	9	3	6	2	5	8	4	1
5	6	8	1	3	4	2	9	7
9	7	6	4	5	8	1	3	2
3	1	5	2	9	7	6	8	4
4	8	2	3	1	6	9	7	5

Easy Sudoku 35

9	3	6	1	5	8	4	2	7
8	1	4	2	3	7	9	5	6
2	5	7	6	4	9	3	8	1
5	4	3	7	6	1	8	9	2
1	7	9	5	8	2	6	3	4
6	8	2	3	9	4	1	7	5
7	9	1	8	2	6	5	4	3
3	2	8	4	1	5	7	6	9
4	6	5	9	7	3	2	1	8

Easy Sudoku 36

[illegible]	3	1	5	4	7	2	6	8
[illegible]	2	7	6	8	9	3	5	1
[illegible]	5	6	1	2	3	4	7	9
[illegible]	4	3	7	9	1	6	8	2
[illegible]	8	9	2	3	6	7	4	5
[illegible]	6	2	4	5	8	9	1	3
6	7	8	3	1	2	5	9	4
3	9	4	8	6	5	1	2	7
2	1	5	9	7	4	8	3	6

Easy Sudoku 37

1	2	8	7	3	4	9	5	6
4	3	6	5	8	9	7	1	2
5	7	9	6	1	2	3	4	8
2	5	1	3	9	6	8	7	4
6	9	7	8	4	1	2	3	5
3	8	4	2	5	7	6	9	1
7	1	3	4	2	8	5	6	9
8	4	5	9	6	3	1	2	7
9	6	2	1	7	5	4	8	3

Easy Sudoku 38

2	4	1	8	3	6	9	5	7
3	9	6	7	1	5	2	4	8
5	7	8	9	4	2	6	1	3
4	6	3	5	2	7	1	8	9
8	1	5	3	6	9	7	2	4
7	2	9	1	8	4	3	6	5
6	5	7	2	9	8	4	3	1
9	3	2	4	5	1	8	7	6
1	8	4	6	7	3	5	9	2

Easy Sudoku 39

2	9	4	8	1	5	7	3	6
6	1	5	7	9	3	8	4	2
3	7	8	2	6	4	9	1	5
9	3	6	1	8	7	2	5	4
4	8	2	3	5	9	6	7	1
7	5	1	4	2	6	3	8	9
1	6	7	5	3	2	4	9	8
5	4	9	6	7	8	1	2	3
8	2	3	9	4	1	5	6	7

Easy Sudoku 40

4	9	5	7	1	6	2	3	8
6	2	1	8	3	4	9	7	5
3	8	7	9	2	5	1	4	6
8	7	2	6	5	1	4	9	3
5	1	4	2	9	3	6	8	7
9	3	6	4	7	8	5	1	2
1	4	8	3	6	2	7	5	9
7	6	3	5	4	9	8	2	1
2	5	9	1	8	7	3	6	4

Easy Sudoku 41

1	3	7	2	4	8	6	5	9
2	9	5	1	3	6	7	8	4
6	4	8	5	7	9	3	1	2
3	7	1	4	2	5	9	6	8
8	5	9	3	6	7	2	4	1
4	6	2	8	9	1	5	7	3
7	1	3	9	5	4	8	2	6
5	2	4	6	8	3	1	9	7
9	8	6	7	1	2	4	3	5

Easy Sudoku 42

8	5	7	6	4	1	9	2	3
6	3	9	5	8	2	7	1	4
1	2	4	7	3	9	5	6	8
9	7	2	1	6	4	8	3	5
3	8	6	9	2	5	4	7	1
4	1	5	3	7	8	2	9	6
5	9	3	4	1	7	6	8	2
2	4	1	8	9	6	3	5	7
7	6	8	2	5	3	1	4	9

Easy Sudoku 43

8	1	5	2	9	6	4	3	7
9	6	3	5	7	4	1	8	2
7	2	4	8	1	3	9	5	6
1	7	8	3	2	5	6	9	4
2	3	6	9	4	8	7	1	5
4	5	9	7	6	1	8	2	3
3	4	7	1	5	9	2	6	8
5	9	2	6	8	7	3	4	1
6	8	1	4	3	2	5	7	9

Easy Sudoku 44

9	2	4	1	3	6	5	8	7
1	3	5	7	4	8	2	6	9
6	7	8	9	2	5	1	3	4
4	6	3	2	7	1	8	9	5
5	9	7	8	6	4	3	1	2
8	1	2	5	9	3	7	4	6
2	4	1	6	8	7	9	5	3
7	5	6	3	1	9	4	2	8
3	8	9	4	5	2	6	7	1

Easy Sudoku 45

3	8	1	7	9	6	4	5	2
2	4	9	8	5	1	3	7	6
5	6	7	2	3	4	8	9	1
8	5	2	3	1	9	7	6	4
9	3	4	6	2	7	1	8	5
7	1	6	4	8	5	9	2	3
6	7	5	9	4	3	2	1	8
1	2	3	5	7	8	6	4	9
4	9	8	1	6	2	5	3	7

Easy Sudoku 46

5	6	9	3	1	2	8	7	4
1	2	7	4	5	8	9	3	6
3	4	8	6	9	7	5	1	2
2	5	4	9	7	6	1	8	3
6	9	1	2	8	3	4	5	7
7	8	3	1	4	5	6	2	9
8	1	6	7	3	9	2	4	5
9	7	5	8	2	4	3	6	1
4	3	2	5	6	1	7	9	8

Easy Sudoku 47

8	3	4	9	2	5	1	7	6
7	1	5	3	4	6	2	8	9
9	6	2	7	1	8	3	4	5
1	7	8	6	3	2	5	9	4
5	9	3	8	7	4	6	2	1
2	4	6	1	5	9	7	3	8
6	8	1	2	9	7	4	5	3
3	5	7	4	8	1	9	6	2
4	2	9	5	6	3	8	1	7

Easy Sudoku 48

[illegible]	3	1	6	4	7	9	5	8
[illegible]	9	5	1	3	8	2	6	7
[illegible]	6	8	2	9	5	1	3	4
[illegible]	7	9	5	8	1	6	4	2
[illegible]	2	6	4	7	9	3	8	1
[illegible]	1	4	3	6	2	5	7	9
[illegible]	4	2	7	1	3	8	9	5
[illegible]	5	7	8	2	6	4	1	3
[illegible]	8	3	9	5	4	7	2	6

Easy Sudoku 49

9	2	8	4	6	1	5	7	3
6	3	4	7	5	9	1	8	2
1	5	7	2	8	3	4	6	9
2	4	6	5	7	8	3	9	1
3	7	1	6	9	4	2	5	8
8	9	5	1	3	2	6	4	7
4	8	9	3	1	5	7	2	6
7	1	2	8	4	6	9	3	5
5	6	3	9	2	7	8	1	4

Easy Sudoku 50

9	5	6	3	2	7	1	4	8
7	8	2	4	1	5	3	9	6
1	3	4	6	8	9	2	5	7
5	2	8	7	3	4	9	6	1
3	4	9	5	6	1	7	8	2
6	7	1	2	9	8	5	3	4
8	6	3	1	5	2	4	7	9
2	9	7	8	4	3	6	1	5
4	1	5	9	7	6	8	2	3

Easy Sudoku 51

6	7	9	3	2	8	4	5	1
8	2	4	9	1	5	3	6	7
3	5	1	6	7	4	2	8	9
4	9	8	7	6	2	5	1	3
1	3	5	4	8	9	6	7	2
2	6	7	5	3	1	8	9	4
5	1	2	8	9	3	7	4	6
7	4	3	1	5	6	9	2	8
9	8	6	2	4	7	1	3	5

Easy Sudoku 52

4	6	1	3	8	9	7	2	5
3	9	5	2	1	7	8	4	6
8	2	7	4	5	6	9	3	1
1	3	9	5	4	8	2	6	7
6	4	2	7	9	3	1	5	8
5	7	8	6	2	1	4	9	3
7	5	4	8	6	2	3	1	9
9	8	6	1	3	4	5	7	2
2	1	3	9	7	5	6	8	4

Easy Sudoku 53

8	6	3	9	1	4	5	2	7
4	2	9	7	5	8	3	6	1
1	5	7	2	3	6	8	9	4
5	3	4	8	6	7	2	1	9
2	8	6	3	9	1	4	7	5
7	9	1	4	2	5	6	3	8
9	4	2	1	8	3	7	5	6
6	1	8	5	7	2	9	4	3
3	7	5	6	4	9	1	8	2

Easy Sudoku 54

7	2	4	1	3	6	9	5	8
8	6	3	9	2	5	1	4	7
9	5	1	4	7	8	2	3	6
4	7	2	6	5	9	3	8	1
1	9	5	7	8	3	4	6	2
3	8	6	2	1	4	5	7	9
2	1	8	5	4	7	6	9	3
5	3	9	8	6	2	7	1	4
6	4	7	3	9	1	8	2	5

Easy Sudoku 55

9	2	3	8	4	6	1	5	
8	1	5	9	3	7	6	2	4
4	6	7	5	1	2	8	9	3
1	7	6	2	5	8	3	4	9
5	8	4	1	9	3	7	6	2
2	3	9	6	7	4	5	1	8
3	4	2	7	6	5	9	8	1
6	9	8	3	2	1	4	7	5
7	5	1	4	8	9	2	3	6

Easy Sudoku 56

2	4	9	8	5	1	6	7	3
7	5	3	6	4	9	1	8	2
6	8	1	2	7	3	9	4	5
8	3	4	7	9	6	2	5	1
5	9	6	1	8	2	4	3	7
1	7	2	4	3	5	8	6	9
9	2	7	3	6	8	5	1	4
3	6	5	9	1	4	7	2	8
4	1	8	5	2	7	3	9	6

Easy Sudoku 57

8	5	2	4	9	3	7	1	6
6	3	9	5	1	7	8	2	4
1	7	4	6	8	2	3	5	9
2	6	8	1	7	4	5	9	3
5	4	3	9	2	8	1	6	7
7	9	1	3	5	6	2	4	8
9	8	5	7	6	1	4	3	2
3	2	6	8	4	5	9	7	1
4	1	7	2	3	9	6	8	5

Easy Sudoku 58

6	1	7	8	3	9	2	4	5
8	3	5	2	1	4	6	7	9
4	9	2	6	5	7	3	8	1
9	5	6	3	2	8	4	1	7
1	8	3	7	4	6	5	9	2
7	2	4	5	9	1	8	3	6
3	6	1	4	7	5	9	2	8
5	4	9	1	8	2	7	6	3
2	7	8	9	6	3	1	5	4

Easy Sudoku 59

5	9	7	6	4	8	2	1	3
3	8	2	5	1	7	4	6	9
1	4	6	2	9	3	8	5	7
4	6	9	3	2	1	5	7	8
2	5	1	8	7	4	9	3	6
7	3	8	9	5	6	1	2	4
6	2	3	1	8	9	7	4	5
8	1	4	7	6	5	3	9	2
9	7	5	4	3	2	6	8	1

Easy Sudoku 60

2	3	4	6	5	9	8	1
5	9	7	8	1	2	6	3
6	1	3	9	2	7	4	5
7	4	8	2	3	1	9	6
3	6	1	5	4	8	7	2
8	2	6	7	9	3	5	4
1	7	5	3	8	4	2	9
4	8	9	1	6	5	3	7
9	5	2	4	7	6	1	8

Easy Sudoku 61

6	1	9	5	2	3	8	7	4
7	8	2	1	6	4	5	9	3
3	4	5	7	8	9	6	1	2
8	5	3	4	7	6	9	2	1
1	9	7	8	5	2	3	4	6
2	6	4	9	3	1	7	8	5
9	7	6	2	1	5	4	3	8
4	3	1	6	9	8	2	5	7
5	2	8	3	4	7	1	6	9

Easy Sudoku 62

6	9	3	8	2	4	7	1	5
4	7	2	5	1	6	9	8	3
5	8	1	7	9	3	2	4	6
7	2	6	9	4	5	1	3	8
9	5	8	1	3	2	4	6	7
1	3	4	6	8	7	5	9	2
8	6	9	2	5	1	3	7	4
2	4	7	3	6	9	8	5	1
3	1	5	4	7	8	6	2	9

Easy Sudoku 63

2	8	4	3	1	5	7	9	6
1	3	7	2	6	9	4	8	5
5	6	9	7	8	4	1	2	3
9	2	8	4	3	1	5	6	7
3	7	6	5	9	2	8	1	4
4	5	1	6	7	8	2	3	9
6	9	5	8	2	7	3	4	1
7	1	2	9	4	3	6	5	8
8	4	3	1	5	6	9	7	2

Easy Sudoku 64

1	7	6	8	2	4	9	3	5
8	4	3	6	9	5	7	1	2
9	2	5	7	1	3	4	6	8
4	8	9	1	3	6	2	5	7
2	3	7	9	5	8	1	4	6
5	6	1	2	4	7	8	9	3
3	9	8	4	6	2	5	7	1
6	1	2	5	7	9	3	8	4
7	5	4	3	8	1	6	2	9

Easy Sudoku 65

8	4	9	7	2	5	6	3	1
3	6	5	8	4	1	9	2	7
2	7	1	6	3	9	4	8	5
7	8	2	4	9	3	1	5	6
1	5	4	2	6	8	3	7	9
9	3	6	1	5	7	8	4	2
4	9	8	5	7	6	2	1	3
5	2	3	9	1	4	7	6	8
6	1	7	3	8	2	5	9	4

Easy Sudoku 66

8	2	4	1	6	5	3	9	7
7	9	1	3	4	2	8	5	6
3	5	6	8	7	9	2	1	4
9	8	7	2	3	4	1	6	5
1	3	2	5	9	6	4	7	8
4	6	5	7	8	1	9	2	3
2	4	8	9	5	7	6	3	1
5	1	3	6	2	8	7	4	9
6	7	9	4	1	3	5	8	2

Easy Sudoku 67

4	5	9	3	6	1	7	8	
6	1	2	8	7	4	9	3	
3	7	8	2	9	5	1	4	
1	9	3	5	2	7	8	6	
7	8	6	4	1	3	5	2	
2	4	5	9	8	6	3	7	
5	2	4	1	3	8	6	9	
8	6	1	7	4	9	2	5	
9	3	7	6	5	2	4	1	

Easy Sudoku 68

6	9	2	8	5	3	7	1	4
3	4	5	6	7	1	8	9	2
1	7	8	2	9	4	3	5	6
7	8	4	1	2	6	9	3	5
9	2	6	3	8	5	1	4	7
5	1	3	9	4	7	6	2	8
2	3	1	4	6	8	5	7	9
8	5	9	7	3	2	4	6	1
4	6	7	5	1	9	2	8	3

Easy Sudoku 69

6	5	9	2	8	3	7	1	4
1	7	2	4	5	6	8	9	3
8	3	4	9	7	1	5	6	2
9	2	5	6	1	7	4	3	8
3	4	6	8	2	5	9	7	1
7	1	8	3	9	4	6	2	5
5	6	3	7	4	2	1	8	9
2	9	1	5	6	8	3	4	7
4	8	7	1	3	9	2	5	6

Easy Sudoku 70

9	8	3	4	1	7	6	5	2
4	5	1	6	2	8	7	3	9
6	2	7	5	9	3	8	1	4
7	1	6	8	3	4	9	2	5
8	3	2	9	7	5	1	4	6
5	9	4	1	6	2	3	7	8
3	7	9	2	5	6	4	8	1
1	4	5	7	8	9	2	6	3
2	6	8	3	4	1	5	9	7

Easy Sudoku 71

5	1	3	8	9	4	7	2	6
6	9	2	1	5	7	3	4	8
4	7	8	6	3	2	1	9	5
7	2	4	9	1	6	5	8	3
3	6	5	2	7	8	4	1	9
9	8	1	3	4	5	2	6	7
8	3	7	4	2	9	6	5	1
1	4	6	5	8	3	9	7	2
2	5	9	7	6	1	8	3	4

Easy Sudoku 72

[illegible]	1	6	9	5	7	2	3	8
[illegible]	7	8	1	6	2	4	5	9
[illegible]	9	2	4	3	8	6	7	1
[illegible]	4	3	5	1	6	8	9	2
[illegible]	8	5	2	7	4	3	1	6
[illegible]	2	1	3	8	9	5	4	7
3	3	4	6	9	1	7	2	5
[illegible]	5	7	8	2	3	9	6	4
2	6	9	7	4	5	1	8	3

Easy Sudoku 73

7	9	6	1	2	4	8	3	5
1	8	3	7	5	6	2	4	9
2	4	5	3	8	9	1	6	7
8	6	2	9	3	7	5	1	4
9	3	1	6	4	5	7	2	8
4	5	7	8	1	2	3	9	6
3	7	8	4	9	1	6	5	2
5	1	4	2	6	8	9	7	3
6	2	9	5	7	3	4	8	1

Easy Sudoku 74

6	3	5	1	2	8	7	4	9
1	9	7	3	4	6	2	5	8
8	2	4	5	7	9	3	1	6
2	1	9	8	5	3	4	6	7
5	6	3	4	9	7	8	2	1
4	7	8	2	6	1	5	9	3
9	8	2	6	3	4	1	7	5
3	4	6	7	1	5	9	8	2
7	5	1	9	8	2	6	3	4

Easy Sudoku 75

3	9	1	7	4	6	8	5	2
2	8	6	9	1	5	4	3	7
4	5	7	8	2	3	1	6	9
5	2	8	3	7	9	6	4	1
6	1	3	4	5	2	7	9	8
7	4	9	6	8	1	5	2	3
8	3	5	1	9	4	2	7	6
9	7	4	2	6	8	3	1	5
1	6	2	5	3	7	9	8	4

Easy Sudoku 76

4	5	8	3	6	9	1	7	2
7	6	2	8	1	4	3	9	5
9	1	3	2	5	7	6	8	4
5	7	6	9	2	3	4	1	8
8	3	9	4	7	1	2	5	6
1	2	4	5	8	6	7	3	9
2	4	7	1	9	8	5	6	3
3	9	1	6	4	5	8	2	7
6	8	5	7	3	2	9	4	1

Easy Sudoku 77

7	1	2	8	9	3	5	6	4
4	9	5	2	1	6	8	7	3
6	8	3	4	5	7	9	1	2
8	2	6	7	4	9	3	5	1
3	4	1	6	8	5	2	9	7
5	7	9	3	2	1	6	4	8
9	3	4	5	7	2	1	8	6
1	6	7	9	3	8	4	2	5
2	5	8	1	6	4	7	3	9

Easy Sudoku 78

7	6	4	8	2	5	1	9	3
8	1	2	9	3	6	5	4	7
5	9	3	4	7	1	6	8	2
4	7	8	5	6	2	3	1	9
6	3	1	7	4	9	2	5	8
9	2	5	1	8	3	4	7	6
1	4	6	2	9	8	7	3	5
3	5	9	6	1	7	8	2	4
2	8	7	3	5	4	9	6	1

Easy Sudoku 79

3	9	8	5	4	6	7	1	2
2	6	1	7	8	9	3	5	4
4	7	5	2	3	1	6	8	9
5	2	9	4	6	7	1	3	8
7	1	4	8	5	3	2	9	6
6	8	3	9	1	2	4	7	5
8	4	2	1	7	5	9	6	3
9	3	7	6	2	8	5	4	1
1	5	6	3	9	4	8	2	7

Easy Sudoku 80

5	3	8	2	7	9	6	4	1
4	9	7	1	3	6	5	8	2
1	2	6	4	8	5	7	9	3
7	6	2	5	9	3	4	1	8
3	8	4	6	1	2	9	5	7
9	5	1	7	4	8	2	3	6
2	4	3	8	5	7	1	6	9
6	1	9	3	2	4	8	7	5
8	7	5	9	6	1	3	2	4

Easy Sudoku 81

5	4	8	3	6	9	2	7	1
3	6	1	8	7	2	9	4	5
7	2	9	1	4	5	3	6	8
6	9	5	4	1	8	7	2	3
4	8	7	2	3	6	5	1	9
1	3	2	9	5	7	6	8	4
8	7	6	5	9	4	1	3	2
9	1	4	6	2	3	8	5	7
2	5	3	7	8	1	4	9	6

Easy Sudoku 82

2	6	1	9	4	8	5	7	3
4	5	9	2	3	7	6	8	1
3	7	8	1	5	6	9	2	4
5	8	3	6	9	4	7	1	2
6	9	7	3	1	2	8	4	5
1	4	2	7	8	5	3	9	6
7	2	4	5	6	9	1	3	8
9	1	6	8	2	3	4	5	7
8	3	5	4	7	1	2	6	9

Easy Sudoku 83

3	1	5	6	7	8	2	4	9
4	7	8	9	1	2	6	3	5
6	9	2	3	5	4	1	7	8
7	4	1	8	2	3	9	5	6
5	2	9	4	6	1	7	8	3
8	3	6	5	9	7	4	1	2
9	5	4	7	8	6	3	2	1
1	6	7	2	3	5	8	9	4
2	8	3	1	4	9	5	6	7

Easy Sudoku 84

2	5	4	6	1	9	8	3
1	3	2	8	7	5	4	6
6	8	5	9	3	7	1	2
9	6	3	4	8	1	5	7
4	1	6	7	5	2	3	9
3	7	9	1	2	4	6	8
5	9	7	3	6	8	2	4
7	2	8	5	4	6	9	1
8	4	1	2	9	3	7	5

Easy Sudoku 85

4	6	7	1	5	9	8	3	2
8	5	1	6	2	3	7	9	4
9	2	3	7	4	8	5	1	6
7	3	6	8	1	4	9	2	5
1	8	9	5	6	2	3	4	7
5	4	2	3	9	7	1	6	8
6	7	8	2	3	1	4	5	9
2	1	4	9	7	5	6	8	3
3	9	5	4	8	6	2	7	1

Easy Sudoku 86

3	5	6	1	7	2	4	8
4	2	8	9	5	3	7	6
7	8	2	3	4	5	9	1
2	6	3	4	9	7	1	5
9	3	5	2	1	6	8	4
5	1	7	6	8	9	2	3
6	7	1	8	2	4	5	9
1	9	4	7	6	8	3	2
8	4	9	5	3	1	6	7

Easy Sudoku 87

7	3	1	8	9	4	6	5	2
8	9	4	5	2	6	7	1	3
2	5	6	1	3	7	8	9	4
9	6	3	2	7	8	1	4	5
1	4	7	9	5	3	2	6	8
5	2	8	6	4	1	9	3	7
3	8	5	7	1	9	4	2	6
6	1	2	4	8	5	3	7	9
4	7	9	3	6	2	5	8	1

Easy Sudoku 88

6	9	7	4	1	2	8	3
8	7	3	2	5	9	4	6
3	4	6	8	9	5	7	1
9	5	8	1	6	4	2	7
7	2	5	9	3	6	1	8
1	6	2	7	4	3	5	9
2	3	9	5	8	1	6	4
4	8	1	6	2	7	3	5
5	1	4	3	7	8	9	2

Easy Sudoku 89

8	1	4	9	5	7	3	2	6
9	2	6	1	3	8	5	7	4
3	5	7	2	4	6	8	9	1
4	3	8	6	1	9	7	5	2
5	9	2	8	7	4	6	1	3
6	7	1	3	2	5	9	4	8
7	6	5	4	8	2	1	3	9
1	4	9	5	6	3	2	8	7
2	8	3	7	9	1	4	6	5

Easy Sudoku 90

9	8	3	4	1	7	6	5	2
4	5	1	6	2	8	7	3	9
6	2	7	5	9	3	8	1	4
7	1	6	8	3	4	9	2	5
8	3	2	9	7	5	1	4	6
5	9	4	1	6	2	3	7	8
3	7	9	2	5	6	4	8	1
1	4	5	7	8	9	2	6	3
2	6	8	3	4	1	5	9	7

Medium Sudoku 1

5	1	3	8	9	4	7	2	
6	9	2	1	5	7	3	4	
4	7	8	6	3	2	1	9	
7	2	4	9	1	6	5	8	
3	6	5	2	7	8	4	1	
9	8	1	3	4	5	2	6	
8	3	7	4	2	9	6	5	
1	4	6	5	8	3	9	7	
2	5	9	7	6	1	8	3	

Medium Sudoku 2

4	1	6	9	5	7	2	3	8
3	7	8	1	6	2	4	5	9
5	9	2	4	3	8	6	7	1
7	4	3	5	1	6	8	9	2
9	8	5	2	7	4	3	1	6
6	2	1	3	8	9	5	4	7
8	3	4	6	9	1	7	2	5
1	5	7	8	2	3	9	6	4
2	6	9	7	4	5	1	8	3

Medium Sudoku 3

7	9	6	1	2	4	8	3	
1	8	3	7	5	6	2	4	
2	4	5	3	8	9	1	6	
8	6	2	9	3	7	5	1	
9	3	1	6	4	5	7	2	
4	5	7	8	1	2	3	9	
3	7	8	4	9	1	6	5	
5	1	4	2	6	8	9	7	
6	2	9	5	7	3	4	8	

Medium Sudoku 4

6	3	5	1	2	8	7	4	9
1	9	7	3	4	6	2	5	8
8	2	4	5	7	9	3	1	6
2	1	9	8	5	3	4	6	7
5	6	3	4	9	7	8	2	1
4	7	8	2	6	1	5	9	3
9	8	2	6	3	4	1	7	5
3	4	6	7	1	5	9	8	2
7	5	1	9	8	2	6	3	4

Medium Sudoku 5

3	9	1	7	4	6	8	5	
2	8	6	9	1	5	4	3	
4	5	7	8	2	3	1	6	
5	2	8	3	7	9	6	4	
6	1	3	4	5	2	7	9	
7	4	9	6	8	1	5	2	
8	3	5	1	9	4	2	7	
9	7	4	2	6	8	3	1	
1	6	2	5	3	7	9	8	

Medium Sudoku 6

1	2	8	9	3	5	6	4
9	5	2	1	6	8	7	3
8	3	4	5	7	9	1	2
2	6	7	4	9	3	5	1
4	1	6	8	5	2	9	7
7	9	3	2	1	6	4	8
3	4	5	7	2	1	8	6
6	7	9	3	8	4	2	5
5	8	1	6	4	7	3	9

Medium Sudoku 7

4	5	8	3	6	9	1	7	2
7	6	2	8	1	4	3	9	5
9	1	3	2	5	7	6	8	4
5	7	6	9	2	3	4	1	8
8	3	9	4	7	1	2	5	6
1	2	4	5	8	6	7	3	9
2	4	7	1	9	8	5	6	3
3	9	1	6	4	5	8	2	7
6	8	5	7	3	2	9	4	1

Medium Sudoku 8

6	4	8	2	5	1	9	3
1	2	9	3	6	5	4	7
9	3	4	7	1	6	8	2
7	8	5	6	2	3	1	9
3	1	7	4	9	2	5	8
2	5	1	8	3	4	7	6
4	6	2	9	8	7	3	5
5	9	6	1	7	8	2	4
8	7	3	5	4	9	6	1

Medium Sudoku 9

3	9	8	5	4	6	7	1	2
2	6	1	7	8	9	3	5	4
4	7	5	2	3	1	6	8	9
5	2	9	4	6	7	1	3	8
7	1	4	8	5	3	2	9	6
6	8	3	9	1	2	4	7	5
8	4	2	1	7	5	9	6	3
9	3	7	6	2	8	5	4	1
1	5	6	3	9	4	8	2	7

Medium Sudoku 10

3	8	2	7	9	6	4	1
9	7	1	3	6	5	8	2
2	6	4	8	5	7	9	3
6	2	5	9	3	4	1	8
8	4	6	1	2	9	5	7
5	1	7	4	8	2	3	6
4	3	8	5	7	1	6	9
1	9	3	2	4	8	7	5
7	5	9	6	1	3	2	4

Medium Sudoku 11

1	3	4	9	6	5	2	8	7
2	5	6	7	3	8	9	1	4
8	7	9	4	1	2	3	6	5
5	1	3	2	4	9	6	7	8
4	6	8	5	7	3	1	9	2
7	9	2	6	8	1	4	5	3
6	8	7	1	2	4	5	3	9
9	2	1	3	5	7	8	4	6
3	4	5	8	9	6	7	2	1

Medium Sudoku 12

5	4	8	3	6	9	2	7	1
3	6	1	8	7	2	9	4	5
7	2	9	1	4	5	3	6	8
6	9	5	4	1	8	7	2	3
4	8	7	2	3	6	5	1	9
1	3	2	9	5	7	6	8	4
8	7	6	5	9	4	1	3	2
9	1	4	6	2	3	8	5	7
2	5	3	7	8	1	4	9	6

Medium Sudoku 13

2	6	1	9	4	8	5	7	3
4	5	9	2	3	7	6	8	[illegible]
3	7	8	1	5	6	9	2	4
5	8	3	6	9	4	7	1	2
6	9	7	3	1	2	8	4	5
1	4	2	7	8	5	3	9	6
7	2	4	5	6	9	1	3	8
9	1	6	8	2	3	4	5	7
8	3	5	4	7	1	2	6	9

Medium Sudoku 14

3	1	5	6	7	8	2	4	9
4	7	8	9	1	2	6	3	5
6	9	2	3	5	4	1	7	8
7	4	1	8	2	3	9	5	6
5	2	9	4	6	1	7	8	3
8	3	6	5	9	7	4	1	2
9	5	4	7	8	6	3	2	1
1	6	7	2	3	5	8	9	4
2	8	3	1	4	9	5	6	7

Medium Sudoku 15

7	2	5	4	6	1	9	8	3
9	1	3	2	8	7	5	4	6
4	6	8	5	9	3	7	1	2
2	9	6	3	4	8	1	5	7
8	4	1	6	7	5	2	3	9
5	3	7	9	1	2	4	6	8
1	5	9	7	3	6	8	2	4
3	7	2	8	5	4	6	9	1
6	8	4	1	2	9	3	7	5

Medium Sudoku 16

4	6	7	1	5	9	8	3	2
8	5	1	6	2	3	7	9	4
9	2	3	7	4	8	5	1	6
7	3	6	8	1	4	9	2	5
1	8	9	5	6	2	3	4	7
5	4	2	3	9	7	1	6	8
6	7	8	2	3	1	4	5	9
2	1	4	9	7	5	6	8	3
3	9	5	4	8	6	2	7	1

Medium Sudoku 17

9	3	5	6	1	7	2	4	8
1	4	2	8	9	5	3	7	6
6	7	8	2	3	4	5	9	1
8	2	6	3	4	9	7	1	5
7	9	3	5	2	1	6	8	4
4	5	1	7	6	8	9	2	3
3	6	7	1	8	2	4	5	9
5	1	9	4	7	6	8	3	2
2	8	4	9	5	3	1	6	7

Medium Sudoku 18

3	1	8	9	4	6	5	2
9	4	5	2	6	7	1	3
5	6	1	3	7	8	9	4
6	3	2	7	8	1	4	5
4	7	9	5	3	2	6	8
2	8	6	4	1	9	3	7
8	5	7	1	9	4	2	6
1	2	4	8	5	3	7	9
7	9	3	6	2	5	8	1

Medium Sudoku 19

5	6	9	7	4	1	2	8	3
1	8	7	3	2	5	9	4	6
2	3	4	6	8	9	5	7	1
3	9	5	8	1	6	4	2	7
4	7	2	5	9	3	6	1	8
8	1	6	2	7	4	3	5	9
7	2	3	9	5	8	1	6	4
9	4	8	1	6	2	7	3	5
6	5	1	4	3	7	8	9	2

Medium Sudoku 20

1	4	9	5	7	3	2	6
2	6	1	3	8	5	7	4
5	7	2	4	6	8	9	1
3	8	6	1	9	7	5	2
9	2	8	7	4	6	1	3
7	1	3	2	5	9	4	8
6	5	4	8	2	1	3	9
4	9	5	6	3	2	8	7
8	3	7	9	1	4	6	5

Medium Sudoku 21

3	5	8	2	7	9	4	6	1
7	4	9	3	6	1	5	2	8
1	6	2	4	5	8	7	3	9
4	9	3	7	1	2	8	5	6
2	7	1	5	8	6	3	9	4
6	8	5	9	3	4	1	7	2
5	1	4	6	2	3	9	8	7
8	3	6	1	9	7	2	4	5
9	2	7	8	4	5	6	1	3

Medium Sudoku 22

6	2	1	8	3	7	9	4
7	3	9	5	2	1	6	8
9	1	4	6	7	2	3	5
5	4	7	1	6	3	8	2
1	8	2	3	5	6	4	9
3	6	8	9	4	5	7	1
2	7	6	4	9	8	5	3
8	9	5	7	1	4	2	6
4	5	3	2	8	9	1	7

Medium Sudoku 23

3	4	5	8	2	9	6	7	1
9	2	7	1	6	4	8	3	5
6	1	8	7	3	5	2	9	4
4	5	2	9	7	6	3	1	8
8	6	1	2	4	3	7	5	9
7	3	9	5	8	1	4	2	6
1	7	3	6	9	8	5	4	2
2	9	6	4	5	7	1	8	3
5	8	4	3	1	2	9	6	7

Medium Sudoku 24

7	6	2	8	5	3	9	1	4
3	8	1	4	9	7	5	6	2
4	5	9	2	1	6	3	7	8
5	2	6	3	4	9	1	8	7
8	3	7	5	2	1	6	4	9
9	1	4	6	7	8	2	3	5
6	4	3	9	8	2	7	5	1
1	9	5	7	3	4	8	2	6
2	7	8	1	6	5	4	9	3

Medium Sudoku 25

6	4	8	1	9	5	7	2	[illegible]
3	2	9	8	6	7	4	5	[illegible]
5	7	1	2	3	4	8	6	[illegible]
7	5	2	9	8	6	1	3	[illegible]
4	8	3	7	5	1	2	9	[illegible]
9	1	6	3	4	2	5	7	[illegible]
8	6	5	4	7	3	9	1	[illegible]
1	3	4	5	2	9	6	8	[illegible]
2	9	7	6	1	8	3	4	5

Medium Sudoku 26

7	9	3	8	1	5	4	2	6
6	4	8	9	7	2	5	1	3
5	1	2	3	6	4	7	8	9
8	6	4	1	2	7	9	3	5
1	2	5	4	9	3	6	7	8
9	3	7	5	8	6	1	4	2
2	7	9	6	3	1	8	5	4
3	5	6	7	4	8	2	9	1
4	8	1	2	5	9	3	6	7

Medium Sudoku 27

8	7	5	6	4	1	3	9	2
9	1	3	7	8	2	4	5	6
2	4	6	5	9	3	7	8	[illegible]
3	6	2	8	5	4	9	1	7
7	5	1	9	3	6	2	4	8
4	8	9	1	2	7	5	6	3
1	9	4	2	7	8	6	3	5
5	2	8	3	6	9	1	7	4
6	3	7	4	1	5	8	2	9

Medium Sudoku 28

2	9	4	8	3	1	6	7	5
5	8	6	4	2	7	1	3	9
1	7	3	5	6	9	2	8	4
4	1	7	9	5	8	3	2	6
9	6	2	1	4	3	7	5	8
3	5	8	6	7	2	9	4	1
6	2	1	7	8	5	4	9	3
7	4	5	3	9	6	8	1	2
8	3	9	2	1	4	5	6	7

Medium Sudoku 29

8	4	6	7	5	1	2	9	3
7	3	9	2	6	8	5	4	1
2	1	5	3	4	9	6	7	8
9	5	4	8	2	6	1	3	7
6	7	2	9	1	3	8	5	4
1	8	3	4	7	5	9	2	6
3	6	1	5	9	4	7	8	2
4	9	7	6	8	2	3	1	5
5	2	8	1	3	7	4	6	9

Medium Sudoku 30

[illegible]	1	9	8	7	2	6	3	4
[illegible]	6	8	3	4	9	5	7	1
[illegible]	4	3	1	5	6	9	8	2
[illegible]	7	4	6	9	3	1	2	5
[illegible]	9	2	4	1	5	7	6	8
[illegible]	5	1	7	2	8	3	4	9
[illegible]	3	6	5	8	4	2	1	7
[illegible]	2	7	9	6	1	8	5	3
[illegible]	8	5	2	3	7	4	9	6

Medium Sudoku 31

4	3	7	6	5	8	2	9	1
9	5	6	7	1	2	4	3	8
1	8	2	9	4	3	5	6	7
8	9	4	1	7	6	3	5	2
7	1	3	5	2	4	6	8	9
2	6	5	3	8	9	1	7	4
3	7	9	2	6	1	8	4	5
5	2	8	4	3	7	9	1	6
6	4	1	8	9	5	7	2	3

Medium Sudoku 32

[illegible]	2	8	3	4	9	5	7	1
[illegible]	7	4	8	1	2	6	3	9
[illegible]	3	1	7	5	6	4	8	2
[illegible]	9	2	4	3	1	8	5	6
[illegible]	4	5	9	6	8	7	2	3
[illegible]	8	6	2	7	5	9	1	4
[illegible]	5	3	1	9	4	2	6	7
[illegible]	1	9	6	8	7	3	4	5
[illegible]	6	7	5	2	3	1	9	8

Medium Sudoku 33

7	9	2	6	1	4	8	3	5
3	4	8	2	5	9	7	6	1
6	1	5	8	7	3	9	2	4
8	6	4	3	2	1	5	9	7
9	7	3	4	8	5	6	1	2
2	5	1	7	9	6	3	4	8
1	3	6	5	4	8	2	7	9
4	8	7	9	3	2	1	5	6
5	2	9	1	6	7	4	8	3

Medium Sudoku 34

[illegible]	4	7	9	5	8	3	6	1
[illegible]	6	3	4	7	1	5	9	2
[illegible]	1	5	2	3	6	4	7	8
[illegible]	7	6	8	1	5	2	4	9
[illegible]	5	8	3	9	2	6	1	7
[illegible]	9	2	6	4	7	8	3	5
[illegible]	2	4	1	6	9	7	8	3
[illegible]	8	9	7	2	3	1	5	4
[illegible]	3	1	5	8	4	9	2	6

Medium Sudoku 35

3	8	5	7	4	9	2	6	1
2	4	6	5	3	1	7	9	8
7	9	1	6	8	2	3	4	5
4	1	9	8	2	5	6	7	3
8	6	2	9	7	3	5	1	4
5	7	3	1	6	4	8	2	9
6	3	4	2	1	8	9	5	7
9	2	8	4	5	7	1	3	6
1	5	7	3	9	6	4	8	2

Medium Sudoku 36

5	2	9	8	3	4	1	7	6
4	7	6	2	1	9	3	5	8
1	8	3	5	6	7	9	2	4
9	4	8	3	7	1	5	6	2
6	1	7	4	2	5	8	9	3
2	3	5	6	9	8	4	1	7
3	5	1	7	4	2	6	8	9
8	6	2	9	5	3	7	4	1
7	9	4	1	8	6	2	3	5

Medium Sudoku 37

7	3	4	1	8	5	9	2	[illegible]
8	5	2	9	6	4	1	3	[illegible]
9	1	6	2	7	3	8	4	5
4	9	3	7	1	2	5	6	8
5	6	8	4	3	9	2	7	[illegible]
1	2	7	6	5	8	3	9	4
6	7	5	3	2	1	4	8	9
3	8	9	5	4	7	6	1	2
2	4	1	8	9	6	7	5	3

Medium Sudoku 38

1	7	8	9	5	4	2	3	6
9	2	5	3	6	8	4	7	1
3	4	6	1	2	7	5	8	9
7	5	4	6	3	1	8	9	2
6	9	1	5	8	2	7	4	3
8	3	2	4	7	9	6	1	5
2	1	3	7	4	6	9	5	8
4	6	9	8	1	5	3	2	7
5	8	7	2	9	3	1	6	4

Medium Sudoku 39

2	3	7	8	5	1	6	4	9
9	8	4	7	2	6	5	1	3
1	6	5	9	3	4	7	8	2
3	1	8	6	4	5	9	2	7
6	5	2	1	9	7	8	3	4
4	7	9	2	8	3	1	5	6
5	4	1	3	6	9	2	7	8
7	2	6	4	1	8	3	9	5
8	9	3	5	7	2	4	6	1

Medium Sudoku 40

7	9	1	5	6	3	8	2	4
2	3	4	7	8	1	9	5	6
5	6	8	4	9	2	7	1	3
3	7	9	2	1	6	4	8	5
4	8	2	3	5	7	6	9	1
1	5	6	8	4	9	2	3	7
8	1	3	6	2	4	5	7	9
9	4	5	1	7	8	3	6	2
6	2	7	9	3	5	1	4	8

Medium Sudoku 41

4	5	6	7	9	1	8	2	3
2	9	7	3	6	8	5	1	4
8	1	3	4	2	5	9	7	6
1	4	8	2	5	7	3	6	9
7	2	5	9	3	6	1	4	8
3	6	9	8	1	4	7	5	2
5	3	4	6	7	9	2	8	1
6	7	2	1	8	3	4	9	5
9	8	1	5	4	2	6	3	7

Medium Sudoku 42

1	5	8	3	6	9	4	7
8	3	4	9	5	1	2	6
9	6	1	2	7	5	8	3
2	8	5	4	3	7	9	1
4	1	6	7	8	3	5	2
5	7	9	1	2	8	6	4
6	4	7	8	1	2	3	9
7	2	3	6	9	4	1	5
3	9	2	5	4	6	7	8

Medium Sudoku 43

6	5	8	9	4	2	7	1	3
3	4	9	5	1	7	6	8	2
7	1	2	6	8	3	9	4	5
5	2	4	8	3	9	1	6	7
8	6	1	7	2	4	5	3	9
9	3	7	1	5	6	8	2	4
1	7	3	2	6	5	4	9	8
2	8	5	4	9	1	3	7	6
4	9	6	3	7	8	2	5	1

Medium Sudoku 44

3	5	6	2	9	8	4	1
8	2	5	1	4	9	7	3
1	4	8	7	3	5	2	6
9	6	7	3	2	1	5	4
5	1	4	9	6	7	3	8
4	7	1	5	8	6	9	2
2	3	9	6	5	4	8	7
6	9	2	8	7	3	1	5
7	8	3	4	1	2	6	9

Medium Sudoku 45

9	5	2	3	8	4	1	7	6
1	3	4	6	7	9	2	8	5
6	7	8	5	1	2	9	3	4
7	6	9	1	2	5	3	4	8
5	8	1	7	4	3	6	9	2
2	4	3	8	9	6	7	5	1
3	1	7	4	6	8	5	2	9
8	2	5	9	3	1	4	6	7
4	9	6	2	5	7	8	1	3

Medium Sudoku 46

8	3	4	9	5	2	1	6
4	1	7	6	2	3	5	8
2	6	3	8	1	4	7	9
7	9	8	1	4	5	3	2
3	5	6	2	7	8	9	1
1	2	5	3	9	6	4	7
9	8	2	4	3	7	6	5
5	4	9	7	6	1	8	3
6	7	1	5	8	9	2	4

Medium Sudoku 47

5	4	9	6	2	1	7	8	3
1	8	3	9	7	5	2	4	6
2	6	7	3	8	4	9	5	1
3	7	2	5	1	9	8	6	4
6	9	5	2	4	8	1	3	7
8	1	4	7	6	3	5	9	2
9	2	1	4	5	6	3	7	8
4	3	8	1	9	7	6	2	5
7	5	6	8	3	2	4	1	9

Medium Sudoku 48

4	6	2	1	8	7	9	5	3
5	1	7	9	6	3	2	4	8
8	9	3	2	4	5	1	6	7
2	7	8	5	9	4	3	1	6
1	3	5	8	7	6	4	9	2
6	4	9	3	1	2	7	8	5
9	2	6	4	3	8	5	7	1
3	8	1	7	5	9	6	2	4
7	5	4	6	2	1	8	3	9

Medium Sudoku 49

7	3	5	2	4	8	6	9	[illegible]
4	2	9	5	6	1	7	3	[illegible]
6	8	1	3	7	9	2	4	[illegible]
8	9	6	4	5	7	1	2	[illegible]
1	5	2	6	8	3	4	7	[illegible]
3	4	7	9	1	2	8	5	[illegible]
9	6	4	1	2	5	3	8	[illegible]
5	1	8	7	3	4	9	6	[illegible]
2	7	3	8	9	6	5	1	[illegible]

Medium Sudoku 50

4	3	5	6	1	9	7	8	2
7	6	1	8	2	4	3	9	5
8	9	2	3	5	7	6	4	1
2	7	4	5	3	1	9	6	8
1	5	9	7	8	6	2	3	4
3	8	6	4	9	2	5	1	7
5	1	7	9	4	3	8	2	6
6	2	3	1	7	8	4	5	9
9	4	8	2	6	5	1	7	3

Medium Sudoku 51

8	3	6	5	9	7	1	2	4
4	1	5	6	2	8	7	9	3
7	9	2	3	1	4	5	6	8
6	2	9	4	3	1	8	7	5
1	4	7	8	5	2	6	3	9
3	5	8	7	6	9	2	4	[illegible]
5	7	4	9	8	6	3	1	2
9	8	1	2	7	3	4	5	6
2	6	3	1	4	5	9	8	7

Medium Sudoku 52

9	8	3	4	1	5	6	2	7
2	4	7	3	6	9	8	5	1
5	1	6	2	7	8	3	4	9
3	6	9	5	8	1	2	7	4
7	2	1	9	3	4	5	6	8
8	5	4	6	2	7	9	1	3
1	3	8	7	5	2	4	9	6
6	9	2	1	4	3	7	8	5
4	7	5	8	9	6	1	3	2

Medium Sudoku 53

8	7	4	3	9	2	6	1	5
1	9	2	4	5	6	7	8	3
5	6	3	7	8	1	2	9	4
9	1	7	2	6	3	5	4	8
2	3	8	5	4	7	9	6	1
4	5	6	8	1	9	3	2	7
7	2	9	1	3	4	8	5	6
3	4	5	6	2	8	1	7	9
6	8	1	9	7	5	4	3	2

Medium Sudoku 54

9	2	5	3	4	7	1	8	6
8	4	7	6	1	5	3	2	9
3	6	1	2	8	9	5	4	7
4	1	8	7	2	3	6	9	5
5	3	9	8	6	1	2	7	4
2	7	6	9	5	4	8	1	3
1	5	2	4	9	6	7	3	8
6	9	3	1	7	8	4	5	2
7	8	4	5	3	2	9	6	1

Medium Sudoku 55

2	9	4	7	3	8	1	5	6
3	1	5	2	9	6	4	7	8
6	7	8	1	4	5	9	2	3
4	8	6	9	5	3	2	1	7
5	2	1	4	6	7	3	8	9
7	3	9	8	1	2	5	6	4
8	4	2	3	7	1	6	9	5
1	5	3	6	8	9	7	4	2
9	6	7	5	2	4	8	3	1

Medium Sudoku 56

4	1	3	7	5	8	2	6	9
5	2	7	1	6	9	3	4	8
6	8	9	2	3	4	7	5	1
7	3	1	8	2	5	6	9	4
8	4	5	9	7	6	1	2	3
9	6	2	3	4	1	5	8	7
1	5	6	4	9	3	8	7	2
2	9	8	5	1	7	4	3	6
3	7	4	6	8	2	9	1	5

Medium Sudoku 57

8	2	5	9	4	6	1	3	7
3	6	9	2	1	7	8	5	4
1	4	7	8	3	5	9	2	6
4	8	3	1	6	9	2	7	5
9	1	6	7	5	2	3	4	8
5	7	2	3	8	4	6	9	1
2	3	8	4	7	1	5	6	9
7	5	1	6	9	3	4	8	2
6	9	4	5	2	8	7	1	3

Medium Sudoku 58

1	5	6	7	8	9	2	4	3
7	8	2	4	1	3	9	5	6
9	3	4	2	5	6	7	8	1
3	9	8	5	4	2	6	1	7
2	1	5	6	3	7	8	9	4
6	4	7	1	9	8	3	2	5
8	6	1	9	7	5	4	3	2
4	7	3	8	2	1	5	6	9
5	2	9	3	6	4	1	7	8

Medium Sudoku 59

5	2	3	6	7	1	8	9	4
6	1	7	8	4	9	2	3	5
4	8	9	5	2	3	1	6	7
7	4	1	9	8	6	3	5	2
9	3	2	7	1	5	4	8	6
8	5	6	2	3	4	7	1	9
2	6	8	3	9	7	5	4	1
1	7	5	4	6	8	9	2	3
3	9	4	1	5	2	6	7	8

Medium Sudoku 60

1	9	5	3	4	6	8	2	7
6	4	7	8	2	5	9	3	1
8	2	3	1	7	9	4	5	6
7	3	6	9	1	2	5	8	4
9	8	2	7	5	4	1	6	3
4	5	1	6	8	3	2	7	9
2	7	9	4	6	8	3	1	5
3	1	8	5	9	7	6	4	2
5	6	4	2	3	1	7	9	8

Medium Sudoku 61

8	9	6	7	1	5	4	2	3
3	5	7	6	2	4	8	9	1
1	2	4	8	9	3	6	5	7
5	8	2	9	3	6	7	1	4
4	3	9	1	7	8	5	6	2
6	7	1	5	4	2	9	3	8
9	1	8	3	5	7	2	4	6
2	6	3	4	8	9	1	7	5
7	4	5	2	6	1	3	8	9

Medium Sudoku 62

9	1	5	6	4	8	3	7	2
7	6	2	9	5	3	1	4	8
3	4	8	7	1	2	5	6	9
8	5	1	2	9	6	4	3	7
2	3	4	8	7	5	9	1	6
6	9	7	1	3	4	8	2	5
1	2	6	4	8	9	7	5	3
4	8	3	5	2	7	6	9	1
5	7	9	3	6	1	2	8	4

Medium Sudoku 63

3	6	4	9	2	5	8	1	7
5	9	8	1	7	3	2	6	4
7	1	2	6	8	4	9	3	5
1	8	9	7	3	2	5	4	6
6	3	5	8	4	9	1	7	2
2	4	7	5	6	1	3	8	9
4	5	1	3	9	7	6	2	8
9	7	6	2	1	8	4	5	3
8	2	3	4	5	6	7	9	1

Medium Sudoku 64

9	8	4	2	5	1	7	3	6
7	5	1	6	9	3	8	4	2
2	6	3	7	8	4	9	1	5
5	9	8	3	4	2	6	7	1
4	7	2	5	1	6	3	8	9
3	1	6	8	7	9	5	2	4
6	4	7	9	2	8	1	5	3
8	2	9	1	3	5	4	6	7
1	3	5	4	6	7	2	9	8

Medium Sudoku 65

1	3	5	8	4	6	2	9	7
6	9	2	7	1	5	3	8	4
4	7	8	9	2	3	5	6	1
5	1	6	2	3	4	8	7	9
2	8	7	1	5	9	4	3	6
9	4	3	6	7	8	1	2	5
7	2	9	4	8	1	6	5	3
8	5	4	3	6	7	9	1	2
3	6	1	5	9	2	7	4	8

Medium Sudoku 66

[illegible]	8	7	9	5	3	2	1	6
[illegible]	1	5	2	6	7	3	4	8
[illegible]	3	6	8	1	4	7	5	9
[illegible]	6	2	4	7	5	9	8	3
[illegible]	5	9	6	8	1	4	7	2
[illegible]	4	8	3	9	2	1	6	5
[illegible]	2	4	1	3	8	5	9	7
[illegible]	7	3	5	4	9	6	2	1
[illegible]	9	1	7	2	6	8	3	4

Medium Sudoku 67

7	2	4	8	1	5	9	3	6
5	3	6	2	9	7	1	4	8
8	9	1	6	3	4	2	5	7
6	4	7	9	5	8	3	1	2
9	5	3	7	2	1	8	6	4
2	1	8	3	4	6	5	7	9
1	7	5	4	8	2	6	9	3
3	6	2	1	7	9	4	8	5
4	8	9	5	6	3	7	2	1

Medium Sudoku 68

[illegible]	4	1	6	5	8	2	7	9
[illegible]	6	7	2	4	9	3	8	1
[illegible]	8	2	1	3	7	4	6	5
[illegible]	3	5	9	8	1	7	2	6
[illegible]	1	9	7	2	3	8	5	4
[illegible]	7	8	4	6	5	9	1	3
[illegible]	9	6	3	7	2	5	4	8
[illegible]	5	4	8	9	6	1	3	2
[illegible]	2	3	5	1	4	6	9	7

Medium Sudoku 69

3	5	6	8	2	9	7	4	1
4	7	9	6	1	5	8	3	2
8	1	2	4	3	7	5	6	9
9	2	3	7	5	1	4	8	6
5	4	8	9	6	2	1	7	3
7	6	1	3	4	8	9	2	5
6	8	7	1	9	3	2	5	4
2	9	4	5	7	6	3	1	8
1	3	5	2	8	4	6	9	7

Medium Sudoku 70

[illegible]	5	7	3	6	2	9	8	1
[illegible]	1	6	9	7	8	5	3	4
[illegible]	8	3	4	1	5	2	6	7
[illegible]	4	1	8	9	6	7	2	5
[illegible]	6	2	7	4	3	8	1	9
[illegible]	9	8	2	5	1	3	4	6
[illegible]	2	9	5	8	4	1	7	3
[illegible]	3	5	6	2	7	4	9	8
[illegible]	7	4	1	3	9	6	5	2

Medium Sudoku 71

1	5	2	7	6	4	3	9	8
7	3	4	9	8	2	1	5	6
6	8	9	1	3	5	2	4	7
8	4	6	2	7	3	5	1	9
9	7	5	8	4	1	6	2	3
2	1	3	5	9	6	7	8	4
3	6	1	4	2	9	8	7	5
4	2	7	3	5	8	9	6	1
5	9	8	6	1	7	4	3	2

Medium Sudoku 72

4	6	1	9	7	2	5	8	3
8	7	2	1	3	5	6	9	4
9	3	5	6	4	8	7	1	2
1	4	8	2	5	3	9	6	7
2	5	6	4	9	7	8	3	1
3	9	7	8	1	6	2	4	5
5	2	9	3	8	4	1	7	6
6	8	4	7	2	1	3	5	9
7	1	3	5	6	9	4	2	8

Medium Sudoku 73

5	7	1	6	8	2	3	9	4
9	2	8	4	1	3	6	5	7
6	3	4	5	7	9	8	1	2
1	8	9	7	5	4	2	3	6
2	4	5	3	6	1	7	8	9
3	6	7	9	2	8	5	4	1
7	1	3	2	4	5	9	6	8
4	5	6	8	9	7	1	2	3
8	9	2	1	3	6	4	7	5

Medium Sudoku 74

4	3	5	2	8	6	9	1	7
2	6	7	5	9	1	8	3	4
1	8	9	7	3	4	6	2	5
9	4	6	3	5	7	1	8	2
8	5	2	4	1	9	3	7	6
3	7	1	6	2	8	4	5	9
6	1	4	8	7	5	2	9	3
5	2	8	9	4	3	7	6	1
7	9	3	1	6	2	5	4	8

Medium Sudoku 75

7	6	5	1	2	4	8	3	9
8	1	3	7	5	9	4	2	6
9	2	4	3	6	8	1	5	7
4	5	1	9	7	3	2	6	8
2	9	6	8	1	5	7	4	3
3	7	8	2	4	6	5	9	1
5	3	9	4	8	1	6	7	2
1	4	2	6	9	7	3	8	5
6	8	7	5	3	2	9	1	4

Medium Sudoku 76

8	5	2	4	1	3	9	7	6
3	6	7	5	2	9	8	1	4
9	1	4	6	7	8	3	5	2
1	7	9	8	4	6	2	3	5
2	8	6	3	5	7	4	9	1
5	4	3	1	9	2	6	8	7
4	2	1	9	3	5	7	6	8
6	3	5	7	8	4	1	2	9
7	9	8	2	6	1	5	4	3

Medium Sudoku 77

9	1	7	3	5	2	4	6	8
3	8	2	9	4	6	5	7	1
4	5	6	7	8	1	9	2	3
7	9	5	1	3	8	2	4	6
8	4	3	2	6	9	7	1	5
6	2	1	4	7	5	8	3	9
5	3	4	6	9	7	1	8	2
1	7	8	5	2	3	6	9	4
2	6	9	8	1	4	3	5	7

Medium Sudoku 78

	2	6	3	8	4	7	9	5
3	7	4	9	5	1	8	6	2
5	8	9	2	6	7	3	1	4
9	3	5	1	4	8	6	2	7
6	1	2	5	7	3	9	4	8
7	4	8	6	9	2	1	5	3
8	6	3	4	2	9	5	7	1
2	5	1	7	3	6	4	8	9
4	9	7	8	1	5	2	3	6

Medium Sudoku 79

4	1	7	6	5	8	2	3	9
8	2	5	3	1	9	7	4	6
6	9	3	2	4	7	5	8	1
7	8	2	5	9	3	6	1	4
9	5	1	7	6	4	3	2	8
3	4	6	1	8	2	9	5	7
1	3	9	4	7	5	8	6	2
5	7	4	8	2	6	1	9	3
2	6	8	9	3	1	4	7	5

Medium Sudoku 80

3	7	6	4	2	8	1	5	9
9	4	5	1	7	6	2	3	8
8	1	2	9	3	5	4	6	7
1	3	7	2	8	4	5	9	6
2	9	8	5	6	1	7	4	3
5	6	4	7	9	3	8	1	2
4	2	3	8	1	9	6	7	5
6	8	1	3	5	7	9	2	4
7	5	9	6	4	2	3	8	1

Hard Sudoku 1

9	7	1	5	8	2	3	4	6
3	8	5	7	4	6	9	1	2
4	2	6	9	1	3	5	7	8
7	5	2	8	6	1	4	9	3
1	4	8	3	5	9	2	6	7
6	3	9	4	2	7	8	5	1
8	1	3	6	9	4	7	2	5
2	9	7	1	3	5	6	8	4
5	6	4	2	7	8	1	3	9

Hard Sudoku 2

6	2	1	7	9	4	8	3	5
3	7	4	2	8	5	9	6	1
8	9	5	1	3	6	2	4	7
9	1	6	5	2	3	7	8	4
2	3	7	8	4	9	1	5	6
4	5	8	6	1	7	3	9	2
1	6	3	9	5	2	4	7	8
5	4	2	3	7	8	6	1	9
7	8	9	4	6	1	5	2	3

Hard Sudoku 3

5	1	8	7	4	3	9	6	2
4	6	2	5	9	8	7	1	3
3	7	9	6	1	2	4	8	5
6	9	5	8	3	1	2	7	4
7	2	1	9	6	4	3	5	8
8	4	3	2	5	7	1	9	6
9	8	7	3	2	6	5	4	1
2	5	4	1	8	9	6	3	7
1	3	6	4	7	5	8	2	9

Hard Sudoku 4

5	7	3	8	1	9	6	2	4
8	6	4	2	3	7	1	5	9
1	9	2	6	5	4	7	8	3
9	4	1	3	2	5	8	7	6
6	5	7	9	4	8	2	3	1
2	3	8	7	6	1	4	9	5
3	2	5	4	7	6	9	1	8
4	1	9	5	8	2	3	6	7
7	8	6	1	9	3	5	4	2

Hard Sudoku 5

2	4	7	1	5	8	3	6	9
6	9	8	7	3	2	1	5	4
1	5	3	4	6	9	2	7	8
3	6	1	2	8	5	4	9	7
7	2	4	9	1	6	5	8	3
9	8	5	3	7	4	6	1	2
4	7	9	6	2	1	8	3	5
5	1	2	8	9	3	7	4	6
8	3	6	5	4	7	9	2	1

Hard Sudoku 6

5	9	3	1	6	7	8	2	4
1	6	4	2	9	8	5	7	3
7	2	8	5	3	4	1	6	9
4	1	9	3	2	5	6	8	7
2	3	7	6	8	1	9	4	5
6	8	5	7	4	9	2	3	1
8	5	2	9	7	3	4	1	6
3	4	1	8	5	6	7	9	2
9	7	6	4	1	2	3	5	8

Hard Sudoku 7

5	2	8	1	3	9	6	7	4
3	4	6	5	2	7	8	9	1
7	9	1	4	6	8	3	5	2
4	3	7	2	5	1	9	6	8
6	5	9	7	8	4	1	2	3
8	1	2	3	9	6	5	4	7
9	7	3	6	1	2	4	8	5
1	6	4	8	7	5	2	3	9
2	8	5	9	4	3	7	1	6

Hard Sudoku 8

6	4	7	3	2	8	1	5	9
1	5	9	7	6	4	8	3	2
8	2	3	9	5	1	4	6	7
9	6	5	1	7	3	2	4	8
2	7	4	8	9	5	3	1	6
3	8	1	2	4	6	7	9	5
7	9	6	4	3	2	5	8	1
4	1	2	5	8	9	6	7	3
5	3	8	6	1	7	9	2	4

Hard Sudoku 9

1	8	7	5	3	2	9	6	4
9	6	3	4	7	8	1	2	5
2	4	5	6	9	1	7	3	8
3	5	8	7	6	9	2	4	1
4	7	2	8	1	5	3	9	6
6	9	1	2	4	3	8	5	7
5	1	9	3	8	6	4	7	2
7	3	6	1	2	4	5	8	9
8	2	4	9	5	7	6	1	3

Hard Sudoku 10

[illegible]	7	4	3	1	9	5	8	6
[illegible]	8	1	7	2	6	3	9	4
[illegible]	6	9	4	8	5	1	7	2
[illegible]	9	2	5	6	7	8	1	3
[illegible]	3	6	2	9	8	4	5	7
[illegible]	5	8	1	3	4	2	6	9
[illegible]	1	3	8	7	2	9	4	5
[illegible]	4	7	9	5	3	6	2	1
[illegible]	2	5	6	4	1	7	3	8

Hard Sudoku 11

5	8	9	3	7	1	6	4	2
4	2	1	8	5	6	7	9	3
6	7	3	4	2	9	5	1	8
7	1	5	9	3	4	8	2	6
3	4	6	7	8	2	9	5	1
8	9	2	1	6	5	3	7	4
9	3	4	6	1	7	2	8	5
2	6	7	5	4	8	1	3	9
1	5	8	2	9	3	4	6	7

Hard Sudoku 12

8	1	3	2	4	9	5	7	6
6	7	4	5	3	1	8	9	2
5	2	9	6	7	8	1	3	4
7	4	6	3	5	2	9	1	8
9	3	2	1	8	4	6	5	7
1	5	8	7	9	6	2	4	3
2	6	5	4	1	3	7	8	9
3	9	7	8	6	5	4	2	1
4	8	1	9	2	7	3	6	5

Hard Sudoku 13

8	2	5	4	9	6	1	3	7
7	3	4	5	1	2	6	8	9
9	6	1	7	3	8	2	4	5
1	5	2	6	8	3	9	7	4
4	8	6	9	2	7	3	5	1
3	7	9	1	4	5	8	2	6
2	9	7	3	6	4	5	1	8
6	4	3	8	5	1	7	9	2
5	1	8	2	7	9	4	6	3

Hard Sudoku 14

6	5	8	2	4	9	3	7	1
4	9	3	8	1	7	5	6	2
1	2	7	6	5	3	8	4	9
2	8	4	7	3	5	9	1	6
5	6	1	4	9	8	7	2	3
7	3	9	1	2	6	4	5	8
9	4	5	3	6	2	1	8	7
8	1	2	9	7	4	6	3	5
3	7	6	5	8	1	2	9	4

Hard Sudoku 15

7	8	5	2	1	4	9	3	6
1	9	2	5	3	6	7	8	4
3	6	4	7	8	9	1	2	5
2	7	3	4	6	8	5	9	1
6	4	1	9	5	2	8	7	3
8	5	9	1	7	3	4	6	2
9	1	6	3	4	7	2	5	8
4	2	8	6	9	5	3	1	7
5	3	7	8	2	1	6	4	9

Hard Sudoku 16

3	4	6	9	1	2	7	5	8
2	1	5	8	3	7	9	4	6
8	7	9	4	5	6	1	3	2
9	2	3	6	4	5	8	1	7
1	6	4	7	8	3	2	9	5
7	5	8	1	2	9	3	6	4
4	8	2	5	9	1	6	7	3
5	9	7	3	6	8	4	2	1
6	3	1	2	7	4	5	8	9

Hard Sudoku 17

2	1	5	8	4	9	3	7	[illegible]
3	9	6	5	2	7	8	4	[illegible]
4	7	8	1	6	3	9	2	[illegible]
7	8	2	9	1	6	4	5	[illegible]
5	3	1	7	8	4	6	9	[illegible]
6	4	9	2	3	5	7	1	[illegible]
1	5	4	3	7	8	2	6	9
8	2	7	6	9	1	5	3	4
9	6	3	4	5	2	1	8	7

Hard Sudoku 18

6	2	4	1	8	7	9	3	5
3	5	1	2	9	4	7	8	6
7	8	9	3	5	6	4	1	2
8	1	7	4	6	2	3	5	9
9	4	5	7	3	8	6	2	1
2	3	6	5	1	9	8	4	7
4	7	3	6	2	1	5	9	8
5	9	2	8	7	3	1	6	4
1	6	8	9	4	5	2	7	3

Hard Sudoku 19

6	3	1	7	8	4	2	9	5
2	4	9	5	6	1	7	8	3
5	7	8	9	2	3	4	6	1
7	2	6	1	4	8	3	5	9
4	8	3	2	9	5	6	1	7
9	1	5	3	7	6	8	2	4
3	6	2	4	5	9	1	7	8
8	9	4	6	1	7	5	3	2
1	5	7	8	3	2	9	4	6

Hard Sudoku 20

2	9	5	8	1	6	3	4	7
1	4	7	9	2	3	5	6	8
6	3	8	5	4	7	2	9	1
5	2	9	1	7	8	6	3	4
7	6	1	2	3	4	9	8	5
3	8	4	6	9	5	1	7	2
9	7	2	3	8	1	4	5	6
4	1	6	7	5	9	8	2	3
8	5	3	4	6	2	7	1	9

Hard Sudoku 21

1	6	8	5	7	2	3	9	4
9	7	3	6	1	4	8	2	5
2	4	5	8	3	9	6	1	7
8	5	9	4	6	7	1	3	2
3	1	7	9	2	8	4	5	6
4	2	6	1	5	3	7	8	9
5	8	2	7	4	1	9	6	3
6	9	4	3	8	5	2	7	1
7	3	1	2	9	6	5	4	8

Hard Sudoku 22

[illegible]	6	9	5	4	2	3	8	1
[illegible]	1	4	7	3	6	5	2	9
[illegible]	3	5	8	9	1	4	6	7
[illegible]	7	8	9	6	5	1	4	2
[illegible]	9	2	3	1	7	6	5	8
[illegible]	5	1	2	8	4	7	9	3
[illegible]	4	3	1	5	8	2	7	6
[illegible]	2	6	4	7	9	8	3	5
[illegible]	8	7	6	2	3	9	1	4

Hard Sudoku 23

8	2	7	6	4	5	1	3	9
9	1	4	7	8	3	6	2	5
3	5	6	9	1	2	7	4	8
7	4	2	8	6	1	5	9	3
5	6	9	3	2	4	8	1	7
1	3	8	5	9	7	2	6	4
6	7	5	1	3	9	4	8	2
4	9	1	2	7	8	3	5	6
2	8	3	4	5	6	9	7	1

Hard Sudoku 24

9	5	3	6	1	8	7	2	4
6	1	7	4	9	2	3	5	8
2	8	4	3	5	7	6	9	1
7	6	5	9	8	1	4	3	2
8	3	9	2	6	4	1	7	5
1	4	2	5	7	3	8	6	9
3	2	1	7	4	5	9	8	6
4	7	6	8	2	9	5	1	3
5	9	8	1	3	6	2	4	7

Hard Sudoku 25

9	2	4	7	8	5	1	3	6
8	7	1	9	6	3	2	4	5
6	5	3	1	2	4	7	8	9
2	4	8	5	1	6	3	9	7
3	9	5	4	7	2	8	6	1
1	6	7	8	3	9	4	5	2
4	3	2	6	5	7	9	1	8
7	8	6	3	9	1	5	2	4
5	1	9	2	4	8	6	7	3

Hard Sudoku 26

6	3	1	7	2	8	5	4	9
7	9	4	1	3	5	6	8	2
8	2	5	9	4	6	3	7	1
5	6	7	3	8	1	2	9	4
9	8	3	2	5	4	1	6	7
1	4	2	6	7	9	8	3	5
2	1	8	4	6	7	9	5	3
3	7	6	5	9	2	4	1	8
4	5	9	8	1	3	7	2	6

Hard Sudoku 27

5	9	3	1	6	8	7	2	4
4	6	7	9	2	5	8	3	1
8	2	1	3	4	7	5	9	6
6	3	5	2	7	9	4	1	8
9	1	2	8	5	4	3	6	7
7	8	4	6	3	1	2	5	9
1	5	9	4	8	2	6	7	3
2	4	6	7	1	3	9	8	5
3	7	8	5	9	6	1	4	2

Hard Sudoku 28

9	7	8	4	2	5	1	3	6
4	5	6	8	1	3	7	2	9
1	2	3	9	6	7	4	5	8
7	8	1	5	4	6	3	9	2
2	4	9	3	7	8	5	6	1
3	6	5	2	9	1	8	4	7
8	3	7	6	5	2	9	1	4
5	9	2	1	8	4	6	7	3
6	1	4	7	3	9	2	8	5

Hard Sudoku 29

1	2	5	9	3	6	7	4	[illegible]
6	7	8	2	4	1	3	9	[illegible]
4	9	3	5	7	8	6	1	2
9	1	4	7	5	3	8	2	6
2	8	7	4	6	9	1	5	3
3	5	6	8	1	2	4	7	9
8	4	1	6	2	5	9	3	7
5	3	9	1	8	7	2	6	4
7	6	2	3	9	4	5	8	1

Hard Sudoku 30

9	6	5	4	2	7	1	3	8
3	2	7	1	6	8	5	4	9
8	1	4	5	9	3	2	6	7
6	4	1	9	5	2	7	8	3
5	7	8	3	4	6	9	1	2
2	3	9	7	8	1	6	5	4
7	9	3	6	1	4	8	2	5
1	5	2	8	3	9	4	7	6
4	8	6	2	7	5	3	9	1

Hard Sudoku 31

6	4	5	8	1	2	9	3	7
9	7	1	3	4	5	6	8	2
8	2	3	9	6	7	4	1	5
1	6	2	5	8	3	7	9	4
3	9	7	4	2	6	8	5	1
5	8	4	1	7	9	2	6	3
7	3	6	2	9	1	5	4	8
4	1	9	7	5	8	3	2	6
2	5	8	6	3	4	1	7	9

Hard Sudoku 32

2	4	7	5	6	9	8	3	1
6	5	1	7	8	3	9	2	4
8	9	3	1	2	4	5	7	6
4	1	2	8	5	7	6	9	3
3	6	8	4	9	2	1	5	7
5	7	9	6	3	1	4	8	2
1	2	5	9	7	6	3	4	8
7	8	6	3	4	5	2	1	9
9	3	4	2	1	8	7	6	5

Hard Sudoku 33

8	1	5	2	4	6	9	3	7
3	9	2	5	7	8	4	1	6
4	6	7	9	1	3	5	2	8
9	2	1	6	3	4	7	8	5
5	8	6	7	9	2	1	4	3
7	3	4	8	5	1	2	6	9
6	4	9	3	2	7	8	5	1
1	7	3	4	8	5	6	9	2
2	5	8	1	6	9	3	7	4

Hard Sudoku 34

8	7	5	3	4	2	6	9
2	4	6	8	1	7	3	5
6	5	2	9	7	4	8	1
9	3	7	5	8	1	2	4
1	8	9	4	2	6	5	3
5	2	1	6	3	8	9	7
3	1	8	7	6	9	4	2
7	9	4	2	5	3	1	6
4	6	3	1	9	5	7	8

Hard Sudoku 35

5	6	7	4	1	8	9	2	3
3	2	8	5	7	9	1	4	6
9	1	4	2	3	6	5	7	8
6	4	9	7	5	1	3	8	2
8	3	5	9	2	4	6	1	7
1	7	2	8	6	3	4	5	9
2	8	6	3	4	5	7	9	1
4	9	1	6	8	7	2	3	5
7	5	3	1	9	2	8	6	4

Hard Sudoku 36

5	2	7	4	3	9	8	6	1
9	1	3	8	5	6	2	7	4
4	6	8	7	1	2	9	3	5
6	3	2	5	9	7	1	4	8
8	4	9	1	6	3	5	2	7
1	7	5	2	4	8	3	9	6
7	5	6	9	2	1	4	8	3
2	8	4	3	7	5	6	1	9
3	9	1	6	8	4	7	5	2

Hard Sudoku 37

3	9	2	6	1	4	7	5	8
4	5	8	7	9	3	6	1	2
7	6	1	8	2	5	3	9	4
6	1	7	9	5	2	4	8	3
5	4	3	1	6	8	9	2	7
8	2	9	3	4	7	5	6	1
9	7	6	4	8	1	2	3	5
1	3	5	2	7	9	8	4	6
2	8	4	5	3	6	1	7	9

Hard Sudoku 38

4	9	1	3	8	6	2	5	7
2	5	6	4	7	9	3	8	1
3	7	8	5	1	2	4	6	9
6	2	3	7	9	4	8	1	5
7	8	5	6	2	1	9	3	4
9	1	4	8	3	5	7	2	6
5	3	2	9	6	7	1	4	8
8	6	9	1	4	3	5	7	2
1	4	7	2	5	8	6	9	3

Hard Sudoku 39

1	2	6	4	3	8	9	5	7
5	3	9	7	6	1	8	4	2
7	8	4	2	9	5	1	3	6
8	6	3	9	7	4	2	1	5
2	5	1	3	8	6	4	7	9
9	4	7	1	5	2	3	6	8
3	7	2	5	1	9	6	8	4
6	9	5	8	4	3	7	2	1
4	1	8	6	2	7	5	9	3

Hard Sudoku 40

8	3	7	4	9	1	6	5	2
5	4	9	2	7	6	3	8	1
1	6	2	3	8	5	4	7	9
7	9	3	5	1	2	8	6	4
4	8	1	6	3	9	7	2	5
2	5	6	7	4	8	9	1	3
6	1	4	9	2	7	5	3	8
9	2	5	8	6	3	1	4	7
3	7	8	1	5	4	2	9	6

Hard Sudoku 41

1	2	7	3	4	6	9	5	
5	8	4	7	9	2	1	3	
6	3	9	1	5	8	2	7	
2	4	5	8	6	7	3	9	
3	7	1	4	2	9	6	8	
8	9	6	5	1	3	4	2	
4	1	8	9	3	5	7	6	
7	6	3	2	8	1	5	4	9
9	5	2	6	7	4	8	1	3

Hard Sudoku 42

1	2	3	4	7	8	5	6	9
4	5	7	9	6	2	1	3	8
6	8	9	1	3	5	7	2	4
8	1	6	5	2	7	9	4	3
7	9	2	3	1	4	6	8	5
3	4	5	8	9	6	2	7	1
5	6	1	2	8	3	4	9	7
2	3	4	7	5	9	8	1	6
9	7	8	6	4	1	3	5	2

Hard Sudoku 43

6	4	7	9	2	8	3	5	1
9	1	5	7	3	6	4	2	8
8	2	3	4	5	1	7	6	9
5	3	4	8	1	2	9	7	6
1	7	9	6	4	5	8	3	2
2	6	8	3	7	9	1	4	5
3	9	2	5	8	4	6	1	7
4	5	6	1	9	7	2	8	3
7	8	1	2	6	3	5	9	4

Hard Sudoku 44

4	5	8	3	6	7	2	1	9
6	2	9	1	4	5	7	8	3
7	1	3	8	9	2	6	4	5
8	6	5	9	2	4	1	3	7
9	3	7	5	1	8	4	6	2
1	4	2	6	7	3	5	9	8
3	7	1	4	5	9	8	2	6
5	8	4	2	3	6	9	7	1
2	9	6	7	8	1	3	5	4

Hard Sudoku 45

8	3	7	1	5	6	2	4	9
1	2	4	9	7	8	3	5	6
5	6	9	2	4	3	7	8	1
6	7	2	8	9	5	4	1	3
9	1	8	7	3	4	5	6	2
3	4	5	6	1	2	8	9	7
2	5	1	3	8	9	6	7	4
4	9	3	5	6	7	1	2	8
7	8	6	4	2	1	9	3	5

Hard Sudoku 46

[illegible]	6	7	3	2	9	1	8	4
[illegible]	9	1	4	7	5	2	3	6
2	3	4	8	6	1	7	5	9
[illegible]	7	2	1	3	4	8	6	5
[illegible]	4	8	7	5	6	9	2	3
3	5	6	9	8	2	4	7	1
4	8	3	5	9	7	6	1	2
6	1	5	2	4	8	3	9	7
7	2	9	6	1	3	5	4	8

Hard Sudoku 47

4	2	6	1	9	7	3	5	8
5	3	9	2	8	4	7	1	6
1	8	7	3	5	6	4	9	2
3	1	4	6	7	5	8	2	9
9	6	8	4	1	2	5	3	7
2	7	5	8	3	9	6	4	1
6	4	1	7	2	3	9	8	5
7	9	2	5	4	8	1	6	3
8	5	3	9	6	1	2	7	4

Hard Sudoku 48

8	1	5	9	3	6	2	4	7
3	6	2	4	8	7	5	9	1
7	9	4	5	1	2	8	3	6
6	2	1	7	4	3	9	5	8
9	5	8	2	6	1	3	7	4
4	7	3	8	9	5	1	6	2
5	8	9	6	2	4	7	1	3
1	4	7	3	5	8	6	2	9
2	3	6	1	7	9	4	8	5

Hard Sudoku 49

4	7	1	5	8	3	6	9	2
8	3	9	2	4	6	7	5	1
2	5	6	7	9	1	8	3	4
7	2	8	6	3	4	5	1	9
6	9	5	8	1	2	4	7	3
1	4	3	9	7	5	2	6	8
5	1	4	3	6	8	9	2	7
9	8	2	1	5	7	3	4	6
3	6	7	4	2	9	1	8	5

Hard Sudoku 50

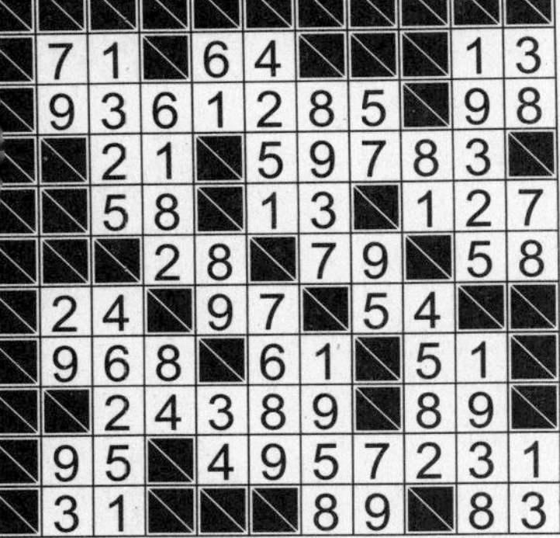

Kakuro 1

	8	4	5	9		5	1		1	3
	7	1	2	3		9	7		4	8
	9	8		4	3	1		4	7	9
		7	9	8	1		8	1		
	1	2	4		7	3	9		5	9
	3	9		3	9	2		2	1	7
			2	1		1	6	9	8	
	3	1	9		8	4	9		2	1
	9	5		9	7		1	5	3	7
	7	6		8	9		7	8	4	9

Kakuro 2

Kakuro 3

Kakuro 4

Kakuro 5

Kakuro 6

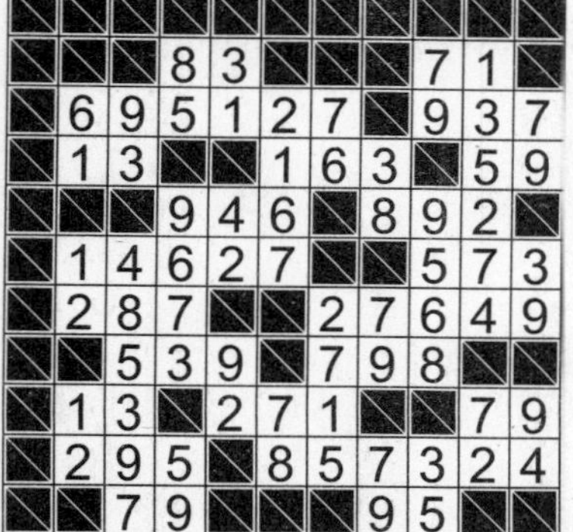

Kakuro 7

3	8			4	1	2			
1	7	8		2	3	6	1	7	
		3	2	1			8	9	
9	8	6	4		1	3		3	9
7	6	9	8		5	7		6	8
3	1		7	9		6	2	8	7
1	2		3	8		2	1	4	3
	3	1			9	8	4		
	5	2	8	3	1		5	1	4
			4	1	2			7	9

Kakuro 8

Kakuro 9

Kakuro 10

Kakuro 11

Kakuro 12

Kakuro 13

Kakuro 14

Kakuro 15

Kakuro 16

Kakuro 17

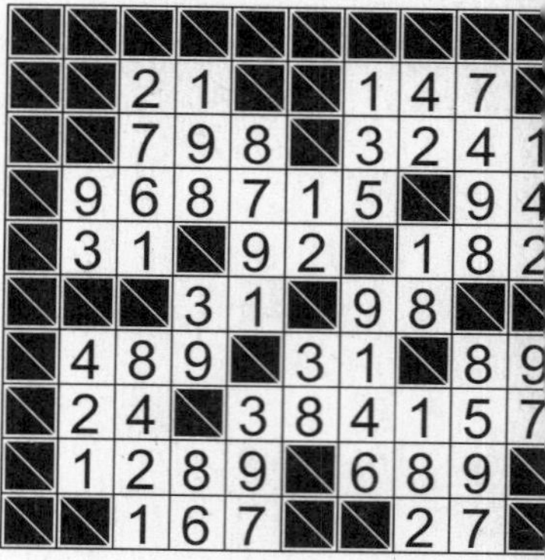

Kakuro 18

Kakuro 19

Kakuro 20

Kakuro 21

Kakuro 22

Kakuro 23

Kakuro 24

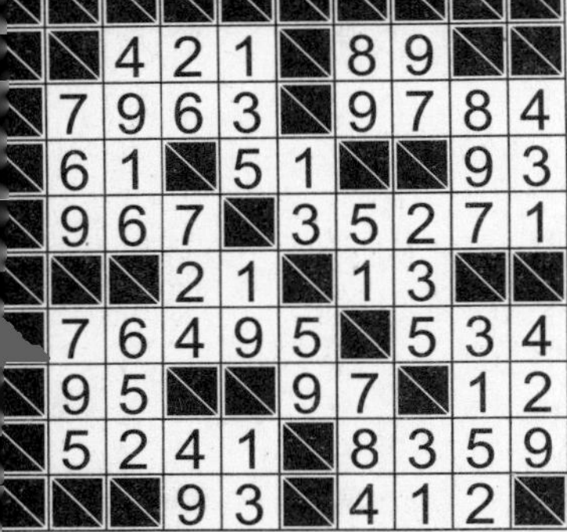

Kakuro 25

	4	5		1	4	7	8		
	2	6		3	1	5	2	7	6
	1	3			9	8		9	8
		4	1	5	2	3			
		8	2	7		6	1	2	
				6	5	9	4	8	
	3	9		3	1			7	2
	1	5	9	8	2	3		3	1
			4	2	3	1		9	4

Kakuro 26

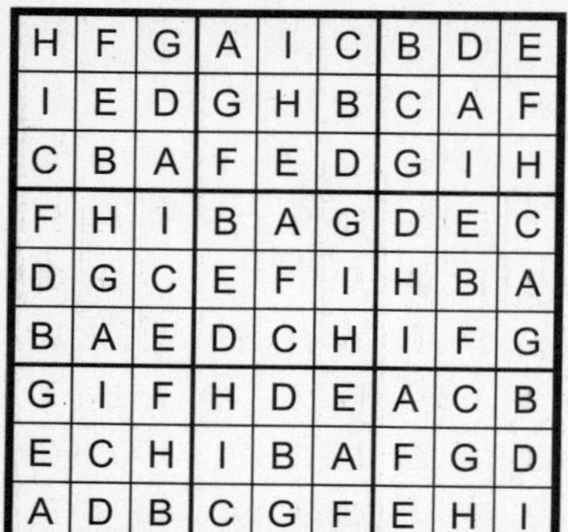

H	F	G	A	I	C	B	D	E
I	E	D	G	H	B	C	A	F
C	B	A	F	E	D	G	I	H
F	H	I	B	A	G	D	E	C
D	G	C	E	F	I	H	B	A
B	A	E	D	C	H	I	F	G
G	I	F	H	D	E	A	C	B
E	C	H	I	B	A	F	G	D
A	D	B	C	G	F	E	H	I

Godoku 1

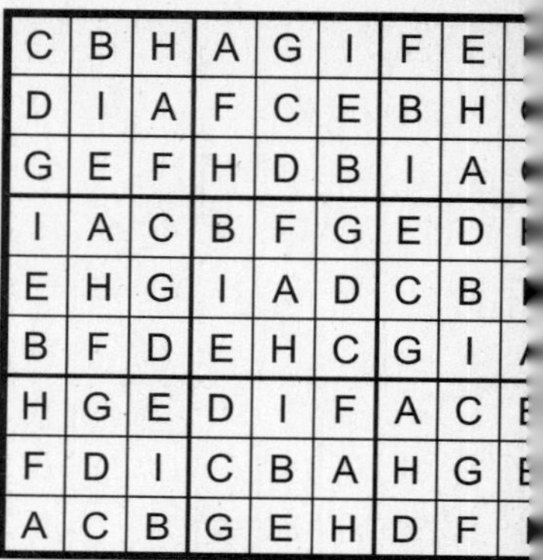

C	B	H	A	G	I	F	E	[illegible]
D	I	A	F	C	E	B	H	[illegible]
G	E	F	H	D	B	I	A	[illegible]
I	A	C	B	F	G	E	D	[illegible]
E	H	G	I	A	D	C	B	[illegible]
B	F	D	E	H	C	G	I	[illegible]
H	G	E	D	I	F	A	C	[illegible]
F	D	I	C	B	A	H	G	[illegible]
A	C	B	G	E	H	D	F	[illegible]

Godoku 2

F	G	B	D	E	I	H	C	A
C	I	D	G	A	H	B	F	E
E	H	A	F	C	B	G	D	I
B	F	E	A	D	G	C	I	H
G	A	H	I	F	C	E	B	D
I	D	C	H	B	E	A	G	F
H	E	I	C	G	F	D	A	B
A	B	G	E	I	D	F	H	C
D	C	F	B	H	A	I	E	G

Godoku 3

C	H	D	G	F	B	A	I	E
G	F	I	C	A	E	D	H	[illegible]
B	A	E	I	D	H	F	C	G
E	C	G	B	H	F	I	D	A
F	I	A	D	E	C	B	G	H
H	D	B	A	I	G	C	E	F
D	G	F	E	B	I	H	A	C
I	B	C	H	G	A	E	F	D
A	E	H	F	C	D	G	B	I

Godoku 4

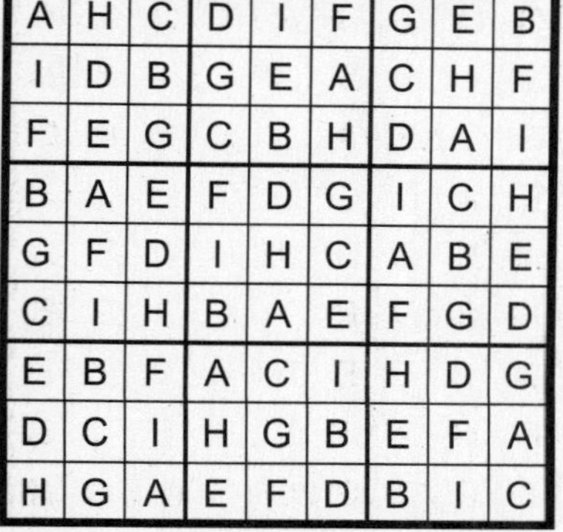

A	H	C	D	I	F	G	E	B
I	D	B	G	E	A	C	H	F
F	E	G	C	B	H	D	A	I
B	A	E	F	D	G	I	C	H
G	F	D	I	H	C	A	B	E
C	I	H	B	A	E	F	G	D
E	B	F	A	C	I	H	D	G
D	C	I	H	G	B	E	F	A
H	G	A	E	F	D	B	I	C

Godoku 5

F	B	C	D	G	E	I	A	H
A	I	D	F	H	C	E	G	B
G	E	H	B	I	A	C	D	F
D	G	I	H	E	F	B	C	A
B	H	A	I	C	D	F	E	G
E	C	F	A	B	G	D	H	I
H	F	G	C	D	B	A	I	E
I	D	B	E	A	H	G	C	F
C	A	E	G	F	I	H	B	D

Godoku 6

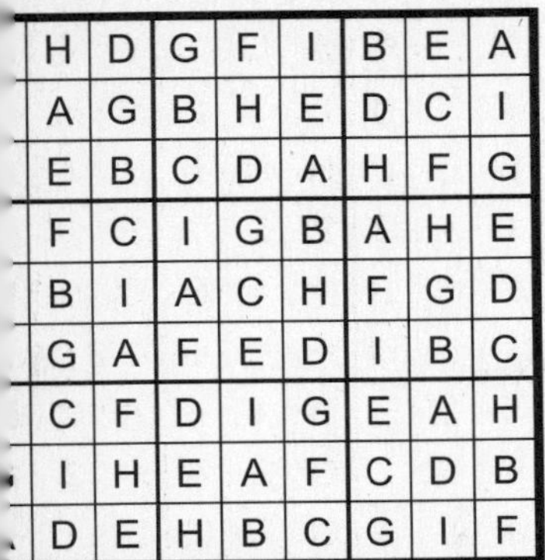

H	D	G	F	I	B	E	A
A	G	B	H	E	D	C	I
E	B	C	D	A	H	F	G
F	C	I	G	B	A	H	E
B	I	A	C	H	F	G	D
G	A	F	E	D	I	B	C
C	F	D	I	G	E	A	H
I	H	E	A	F	C	D	B
D	E	H	B	C	G	I	F

Godoku 7

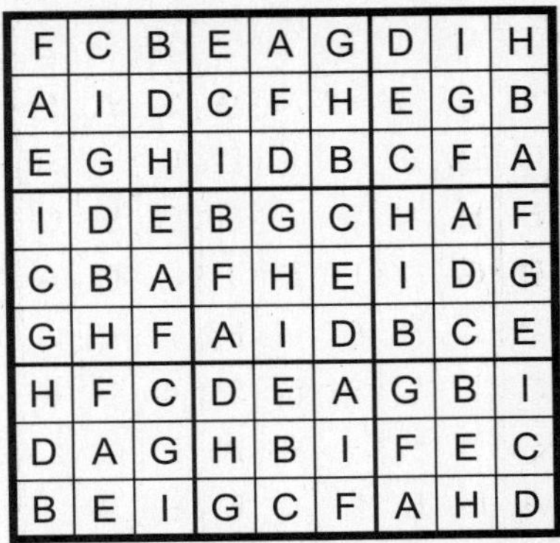

F	C	B	E	A	G	D	I	H
A	I	D	C	F	H	E	G	B
E	G	H	I	D	B	C	F	A
I	D	E	B	G	C	H	A	F
C	B	A	F	H	E	I	D	G
G	H	F	A	I	D	B	C	E
H	F	C	D	E	A	G	B	I
D	A	G	H	B	I	F	E	C
B	E	I	G	C	F	A	H	D

Godoku 8

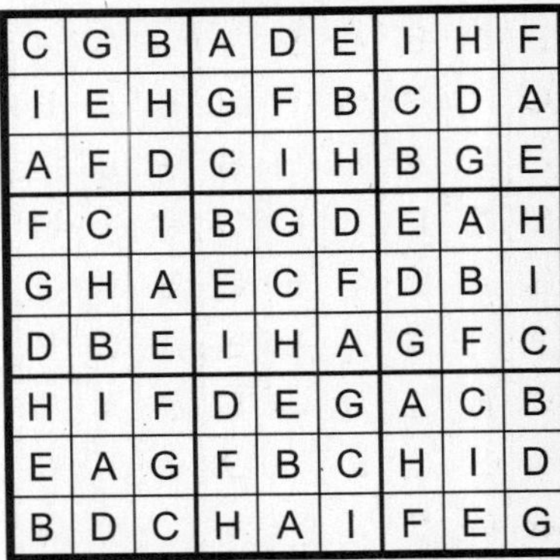

C	G	B	A	D	E	I	H	F
I	E	H	G	F	B	C	D	A
A	F	D	C	I	H	B	G	E
F	C	I	B	G	D	E	A	H
G	H	A	E	C	F	D	B	I
D	B	E	I	H	A	G	F	C
H	I	F	D	E	G	A	C	B
E	A	G	F	B	C	H	I	D
B	D	C	H	A	I	F	E	G

Godoku 10

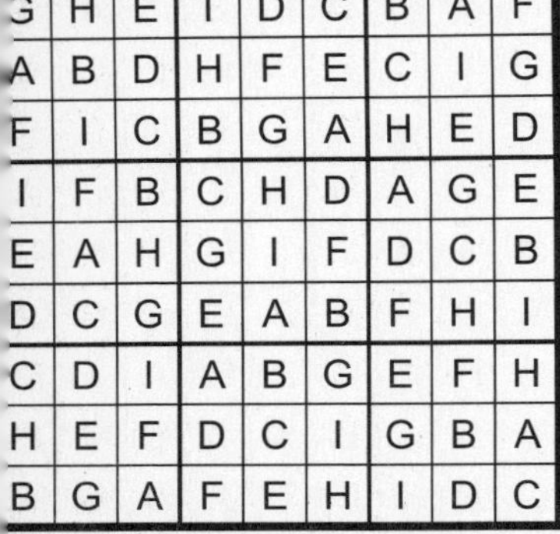

B	C	D	G	F	I	H	A	E
H	E	F	B	C	A	G	D	I
G	A	I	H	D	E	B	C	F
F	G	C	A	B	H	E	I	D
D	H	E	C	I	G	F	B	A
I	B	A	F	E	D	C	G	H
A	F	G	I	H	C	D	E	B
C	D	H	E	A	B	I	F	G
E	I	B	D	G	F	A	H	C

Godoku 9

G	H	E	I	D	C	B	A	F
A	B	D	H	F	E	C	I	G
F	I	C	B	G	A	H	E	D
I	F	B	C	H	D	A	G	E
E	A	H	G	I	F	D	C	B
D	C	G	E	A	B	F	H	I
C	D	I	A	B	G	E	F	H
H	E	F	D	C	I	G	B	A
B	G	A	F	E	H	I	D	C

Godoku 11

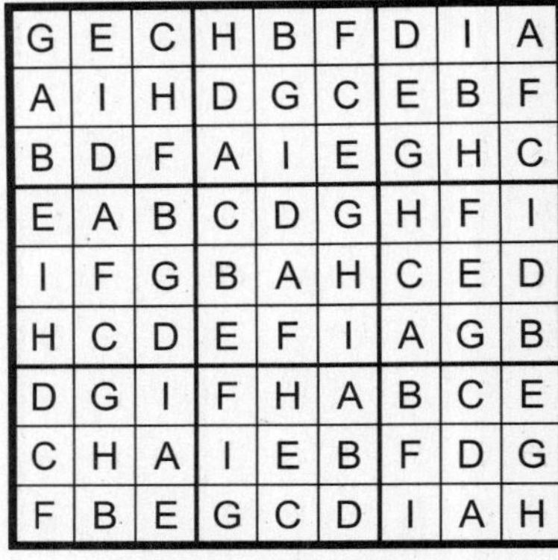

G	E	C	H	B	F	D	I	A
A	I	H	D	G	C	E	B	F
B	D	F	A	I	E	G	H	C
E	A	B	C	D	G	H	F	I
I	F	G	B	A	H	C	E	D
H	C	D	E	F	I	A	G	B
D	G	I	F	H	A	B	C	E
C	H	A	I	E	B	F	D	G
F	B	E	G	C	D	I	A	H

Godoku 12

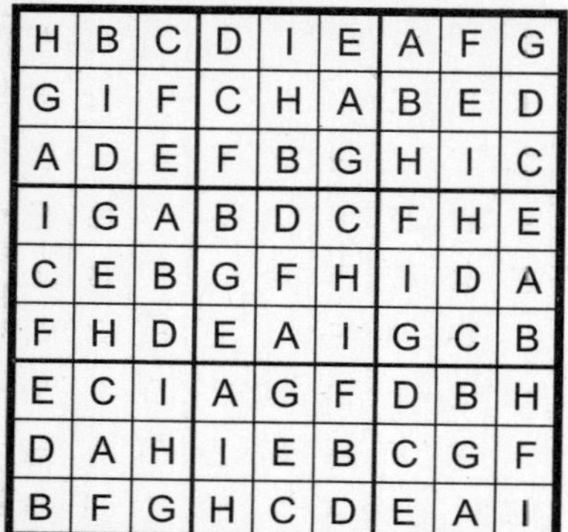

H	B	C	D	I	E	A	F	G
G	I	F	C	H	A	B	E	D
A	D	E	F	B	G	H	I	C
I	G	A	B	D	C	F	H	E
C	E	B	G	F	H	I	D	A
F	H	D	E	A	I	G	C	B
E	C	I	A	G	F	D	B	H
D	A	H	I	E	B	C	G	F
B	F	G	H	C	D	E	A	I

Godoku 13

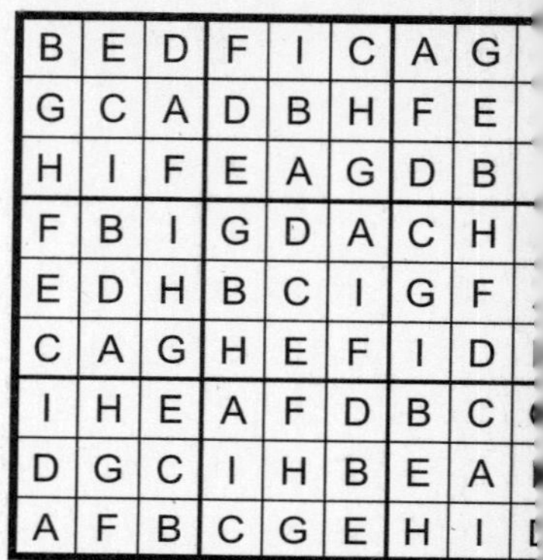

B	E	D	F	I	C	A	G	[illegible]
G	C	A	D	B	H	F	E	[illegible]
H	I	F	E	A	G	D	B	[illegible]
F	B	I	G	D	A	C	H	[illegible]
E	D	H	B	C	I	G	F	[illegible]
C	A	G	H	E	F	I	D	[illegible]
I	H	E	A	F	D	B	C	G
D	G	C	I	H	B	E	A	F
A	F	B	C	G	E	H	I	D

Godoku 14

B	H	G	D	E	C	F	I	A
D	I	F	A	B	H	E	C	G
A	E	C	I	G	F	H	B	D
I	B	A	F	C	D	G	H	E
C	D	H	E	I	G	B	A	F
F	G	E	B	H	A	C	D	I
G	C	D	H	A	E	F	I	B
H	F	I	G	D	B	A	E	C
E	A	B	C	F	I	D	G	H

Godoku 15

G	D	E	I	F	C	A	H	B
B	A	I	D	E	H	G	C	F
F	H	C	A	G	B	I	E	D
A	B	G	H	I	E	D	F	C
I	E	F	B	C	D	H	A	G
H	C	D	F	A	G	E	B	I
C	F	A	E	D	I	B	G	H
E	I	B	G	H	F	C	D	A
D	G	H	C	B	A	F	I	E

Godoku 16

D	E	I	B	F	C	A	H	G
B	A	G	D	H	I	C	E	F
F	H	C	G	A	E	B	D	I
E	G	H	F	D	A	I	B	C
C	D	F	H	I	B	E	G	A
A	I	B	C	E	G	H	F	D
H	C	A	E	G	F	D	I	B
I	F	E	A	B	D	G	C	H
G	B	D	I	C	H	F	A	E

Godoku 17

C	H	D	G	F	B	A	I	E
G	F	I	C	A	E	D	H	B
B	A	E	I	D	H	F	C	G
E	C	G	B	H	F	I	D	A
F	I	A	D	E	C	B	G	H
H	D	B	A	I	G	C	E	F
D	G	F	E	B	I	H	A	C
I	B	C	H	G	A	E	F	D
A	E	H	F	C	D	G	B	I

Godoku 18

F	B	C	D	G	E	I	A	H
A	I	D	F	H	C	E	G	B
G	E	H	B	I	A	C	D	F
D	G	I	H	E	F	B	C	A
B	H	A	I	C	D	F	E	G
E	C	F	A	B	G	D	H	I
H	F	G	C	D	B	A	I	E
I	D	B	E	A	H	G	C	F
C	A	E	G	F	I	H	B	D

Godoku 19

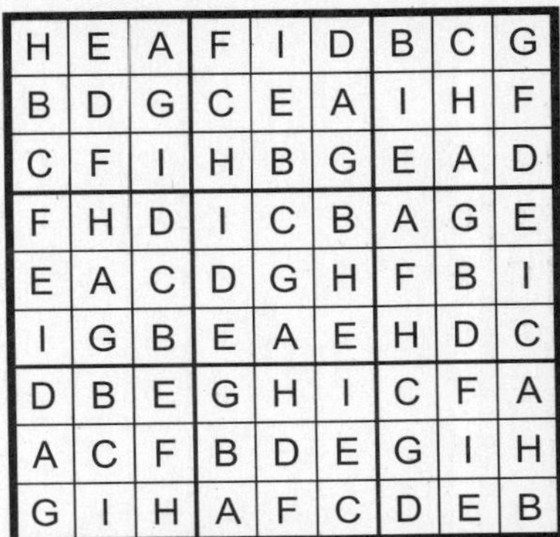

H	E	A	F	I	D	B	C	G
B	D	G	C	E	A	I	H	F
C	F	I	H	B	G	E	A	D
F	H	D	I	C	B	A	G	E
E	A	C	D	G	H	F	B	I
I	G	B	E	A	E	H	D	C
D	B	E	G	H	I	C	F	A
A	C	F	B	D	E	G	I	H
G	I	H	A	F	C	D	E	B

Godoku 20

F	H	A	B	C	D	E	G	I
C	I	D	E	G	H	B	A	F
G	B	E	I	A	F	H	C	D
E	C	B	F	D	G	A	I	H
D	F	H	A	B	I	G	E	C
I	A	G	H	E	C	F	D	B
H	G	F	C	I	E	D	B	A
B	D	C	G	F	A	I	H	E
A	E	I	D	H	B	C	F	G

Godoku 21

A	B	I	C	D	F	G	H	E
D	E	H	I	G	A	C	F	B
C	G	F	B	H	E	I	A	D
B	H	A	E	I	G	D	C	F
G	F	D	H	B	C	A	E	I
E	I	C	F	A	D	B	G	H
F	D	E	A	C	I	H	B	G
H	C	G	D	E	B	F	I	A
I	A	B	G	F	H	E	D	C

Godoku 22

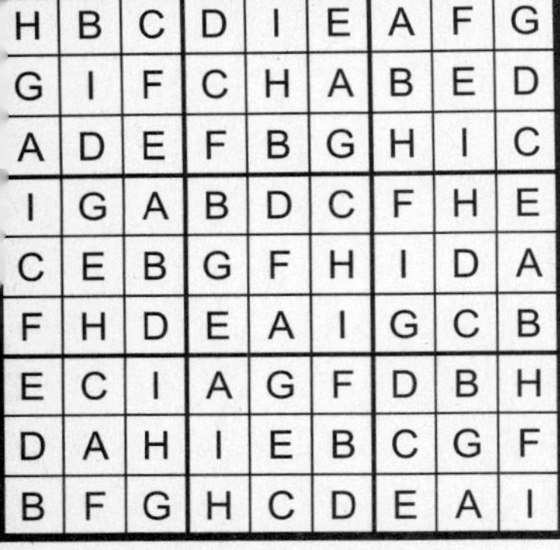

H	B	C	D	I	E	A	F	G
G	I	F	C	H	A	B	E	D
A	D	E	F	B	G	H	I	C
I	G	A	B	D	C	F	H	E
C	E	B	G	F	H	I	D	A
F	H	D	E	A	I	G	C	B
E	C	I	A	G	F	D	B	H
D	A	H	I	E	B	C	G	F
B	F	G	H	C	D	E	A	I

Godoku 23

F	G	B	D	E	I	H	C	A
C	I	D	G	A	H	B	F	E
E	H	A	F	C	B	G	D	I
B	F	E	A	D	G	C	I	H
G	A	H	I	F	C	E	B	D
I	D	C	H	B	E	A	G	F
H	E	I	C	G	F	D	A	B
A	B	G	E	I	D	F	H	C
D	C	F	B	H	A	I	E	G

Godoku 24

G	E	C	H	B	F	D	I	A
A	I	H	D	G	C	E	B	F
B	D	F	A	I	E	G	H	C
E	A	B	C	D	G	H	F	I
I	F	G	B	A	H	C	E	D
H	C	D	E	F	I	A	G	B
D	G	I	F	H	A	B	C	E
C	H	A	I	E	B	F	D	G
F	B	E	G	C	D	I	A	H

Godoku 25